FINE-TUNING THE CLARINET SECTION

A Handbook for the Band Director

Brent Coppenbarger

Published in Cooperation with the
National Association for Music Education

ROWMAN & LITTLEFIELD
Lanham • Boulder • New York • London

Published in cooperation with the National Association for Music Education, 1806 Robert Fulton Drive, Reston, Virginia 20191; nafme.org

Published by Rowman & Littlefield
A wholly owned subsidiary of The Rowman & Littlefield Publishing Group, Inc.
4501 Forbes Boulevard, Suite 200, Lanham, Maryland 20706
www.rowman.com
Unit A, Whitacre Mews, 26-34 Stannary Street, London SE11 4AB, United Kingdom

Copyright © 2016 by Brent Coppenbarger

All rights reserved. No part of this book may be reproduced in any form or by any electronic or mechanical means, including information storage and retrieval systems, without written permission from the publisher, except by a reviewer who may quote passages in a review.

British Library Cataloguing in Publication Information Available

Library of Congress Cataloging-in-Publication Data
Coppenbarger, Brent.
 Fine-tuning the clarinet section : a handbook for the band director / Brent Coppenbarger.
  pages cm
  Includes index.
  ISBN 978-1-4758-2075-1 (cloth : alk. paper) — ISBN 978-1-4758-2076-8 (pbk. : alk. paper) — ISBN 978-1-4758-2077-5 (electronic)
 1. Clarinet—Instruction and study. 2. Clarinet—Construction. 3. Clarinet—Maintenance and repair. I. Title.
 MT380.C67 2016
 788.6'219—dc23
 2015031858

∞™ The paper used in this publication meets the minimum requirements of American National Standard for Information Sciences—Permanence of Paper for Printed Library Materials, ANSI/NISO Z39.48-1992.

Printed in the United States of America

*This book is dedicated to my first clarinet teacher,
my father, Dr. Roger Coppenbarger,
and to my first accompanist,
my mother, Lavonne Coppenbarger.*

CONTENTS

Preface vii

Acknowledgments ix

Introduction xi

  1 The Embouchure 1

  2 The Reed 11

  3 Equipment 19

  4 Maintenance 25

  5 Intonation 33

  6 Articulation 41

  7 Finger Technique 49

  8 Musicality 61

  9 A Colorful Warm-Up Routine 67

  10 Rehearsing the Woodwind Section 75

11	Preparing for a Solo Performance	89
12	Ten Steps to Better Sight-Reading	93

Conclusion	99
Appendix: Additional Materials for Clarinetists	101
Index	107
About the Author	111

PREFACE

As musicians and teachers, we are continually trying to improve our ensembles. Because the clarinet section is so prominent in band music, any improvement in the clarinet section affects the whole band. This book will help the band director develop the clarinet section, and it also includes guidance for the individual clarinet student, from the beginner to the advanced. With a doctor of musical arts degree in clarinet performance, I have studied with some of the finest clarinetists in the United States and have over 20 years of college teaching experience. This text lays out some of my most effective teaching techniques, developed over 37 years of teaching.

Chapter 1 explains the importance of and how to develop a good clarinet embouchure. Chapter 2 talks about the reed and explains the break-in process. Chapter 3 deals with equipment and what to look for when choosing a clarinet, and chapter 4 pertains to the ever-important subject of maintenance.

Chapter 5 examines the critical element of intonation, and chapter 6 speaks to articulation. In chapter 7, finger technique is discussed. Chapter 8 deals with the tricky subject of musicality. Chapter 9 shows a fun warm-up routine that the student can use in the practice room.

Chapter 10 is an informative chapter of rehearsing the woodwind section as a whole. Chapter 11 shows the student how he or she may approach preparing for a solo performance, whereas chapter 12 concludes by explaining my approach to sight-reading.

Throughout the book I have included sections in boxes designated with Beginner, Advanced, or Teaching Tips. This makes for a quick reference guide in each chapter for students or band directors to look up information.

ACKNOWLEDGMENTS

I wish to thank my teachers (in alphabetical order), from whom I have acquired a wealth of knowledge: Glenn Bowen (University of Wisconsin–Madison School of Music), Clark Brody (Chicago Symphony), Roger Coppenbarger (University of Wisconsin-Whitewater), Russ Dagon (Milwaukee Symphony), Anita Garriott (Florentine Orchestra of Italy), Robert Marcellus (Cleveland Symphony, Northwestern University), and Walter Wollwage (Chicago Symphony).

I also wish to thank my father, Roger Coppenbarger, for much of the information contained in the first two chapters of this book.

INTRODUCTION

The amount of knowledge that the band director is expected to have can be overwhelming. He or she is expected to be a teacher, a conductor, an artist, a musician, and an expert on every instrument in the band. Of course, this is very difficult, if not impossible. Musicians spend a lifetime gaining knowledge on their particular instrument or area of expertise and this is an ongoing process. This book is an attempt to give the band director additional information or different ways of thinking about particular areas of interest with regard to the clarinet section of the band.

Clarinets are prominent melody instruments, and a strong clarinet section can make the difference between a good band and a great band. Because of the different levels of abilities and different areas of interest by students, not every part of this book may be appropriate for every student; some chapters are intended to help beginners develop good habits from day one and will be useful for the middle school band director, as well as for the high school band director whose clarinets need to review the basics. Others are intended to help intermediate or advanced students improve their skills. The aim of this book, therefore, is to give the band director some additional tools to improve the clarinet section.

The information contained within this book is based upon many years of lessons with many great clarinetists and many years of teaching great students. One does not only learn from teachers, but one learns from students as well. I had the presence of mind, at a young age, to take notes after my lessons and to file these notes away in a folder. Most of the information and teaching techniques contained here I have incorporated into my own teaching style. Growing up in a home with two university music teachers, talking about music was part of my everyday lexicon.

1

THE EMBOUCHURE

One of the most important aspects of playing the clarinet is tone production. Without a good, characteristic clarinet tone, the student will not be an accomplished clarinetist. The most important part of tone production is the clarinet embouchure. Although a student with a poor embouchure may be able to keep up with a beginning band, his or her problems will increase exponentially as the music becomes more difficult; it is worth the effort to ensure that the beginning student plays with the correct embouchure from day one.

The clarinet embouchure will be discussed with regard to the physical requirements necessary for the instrument to function. This information will be useful for the beginning student, the teacher of beginning students, and the teacher of intermediate students who need review, such as high school students who pick up their instruments in the fall after not practicing much over the summer. It is always easier to learn correctly from the beginning than to repair bad habits at the intermediate level.

There are two types of clarinet embouchures. This chapter will focus on the standard single lip embouchure. The other type of embouchure is the *double lip* embouchure. A few words here with regard to the double lip embouchure.

The double lip embouchure is termed double lip because the top teeth do not touch the mouthpiece as in the single lip embouchure. Rather, the top lip sits between the top teeth and the mouthpiece. This style of embouchure requires a very strong upper lip muscle to prevent the top teeth from cutting into the upper lip. Since setting the teeth on the mouthpiece helps secure the mouthpiece in the mouth, the top lip must take over this function.

This type of embouchure has fallen out of style, with most single reed players preferring the single lip embouchure. However, one may wish to use the double lip embouchure if the two upper front teeth have been damaged and pressure cannot be applied via the front upper teeth to the mouthpiece. Bassoonists and oboists use a double lip embouchure, and a doubler whose primary instrument is a double reed might use a double lip embouchure on clarinet.

A clarinet reed acts much like a suspended lever, opening and closing periodically to close the airway into the mouthpiece, thereby setting up vibrational sound waves within the instrumental column. For discussion purposes, an analogous comparison of the beating reed would be a diving board with the lower lip of the embouchure acting as a fulcrum. To have an efficient diving board one would need a fulcrum placement as shown in figure 1.1. (The arrow points to the fulcrum.)

This leads to the first and foremost factor pertaining to the clarinet embouchure: *placement*. The proper placement of the lower lip, which acts as a fulcrum to the reed, is most critical to clarinet playing. (See figure 1.2.)

The proper distance from the tip of the reed to the fulcrum is approximately 15 to 17 millimeters, depending upon the mouthpiece *lay* dimensions, or where the reed and the mouthpiece part. This places the top teeth about a half inch onto the mouthpiece. Beginners have a tendency to play too close to the tip, because the mouthpiece feels odd to them. The top teeth should touch or sit on the mouthpiece. If one simply blows into the mouthpiece without added pressure against the reed, no sound will be produced.

Figure 1.1. Fulcrum Placement

THE EMBOUCHURE

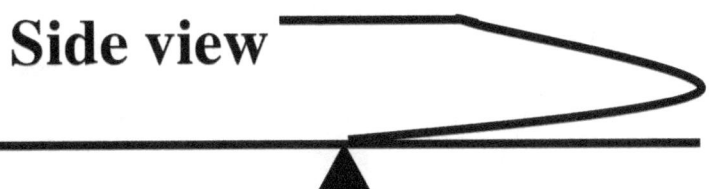

Figure 1.2. Placement of Lower Lip

The lower lip must *load*, that is, slightly bend, the reed toward the mouthpiece. In doing so, the lower lip dampens and slows down the reed's natural tendency to vibrate quickly, about 3,300 cycles per second, allowing it to vibrate in resonance with the pitch being fingered.[1]

However, the lower lip must not over dampen or choke the reed because the reed must have enough freedom to readily change vibrational speed as the length of the clarinet changes (by fingering notes), thus producing different pitches. The reed vibrates in sympathy with the length of the clarinet or the notes fingered. The reed does not *produce* the basic pitch, only the tone. However, the reed can have an influence on the pitch with regard to a note being sharp or flat. This will be discussed in chapter 5.

If the fulcrum or lower lip is too much toward the tip of the reed, the tone will be thin and muffled. If the lower lip is too far back, that is, if there is too much reed and mouthpiece in the mouth, the tone will be loud, bright, and difficult to control and will want to squeak.

The next factor pertaining to the clarinet embouchure is *pressure*. Pressure is also a critical aspect of the clarinet embouchure. The reed must be loaded to the proper amount of pressure. The best way to determine the necessary pressure against the reed is to blow only the mouthpiece and reed.

When the proper lower lip pressure is applied, the resulting pitch will be concert C, a little on the sharp side (about ten cents), but not C-sharp. If too much pressure is applied, the student will have a tendency to play sharp and will lack the ability to play at a forte level; also, the tone will be pinched. If not enough pressure is applied, the student will play flat, the tone will be bright, and the student will have difficulty playing at soft levels.

The *size* and *shape* of the fulcrum (lower lip) are critical. The lower lip must be properly in place, as in figure 1.2, to achieve a good balance.

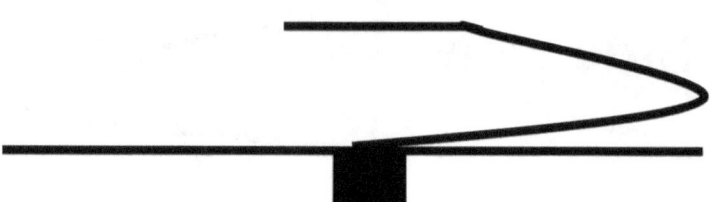

Figure 1.3. Poor Shape for Fulcrum

The fulcrum in figure 1.3 would not function as well as a clarinet embouchure as the fulcrum in figure 1.4. Obviously a sharp edge fulcrum, as in figure 1.1, would not be possible or practical for a lower lip shape. A fulcrum resembling figure 1.4 is possible.

In order to narrow the lower lip and make it stronger, it is necessary to pull the excessive tissue away from the reed by pointing and flattening the chin. Only about half of the red portion of the lip covers the teeth. The reed should not touch the flesh-colored portion of the skin as the muscle of the lip is in the red portion. The corners of the mouth should be pulled inward, like the drawstring of a duffel bag, and the bottom lip should be wrinkled, as if saying *oo* in the word *boo*.

The fourth factor pertaining to the clarinet embouchure is *density*. This factor is more individual, as it depends on each player's natural musculature and mouth shape, especially the thickness of the lips. There is no one-size-fits-all approach to density; each student must find his or her own balance between strength and pressure.

Even if one properly places the correct-sized embouchure, it may not be the most efficient if it is too soft or too hard. A fulcrum of a diving board would be of little value if it were as soft as putty. Likewise, a rock-hard fulcrum with little give will not allow the reed to vibrate properly, or at best it would produce a very harsh tone. The part of the embou-

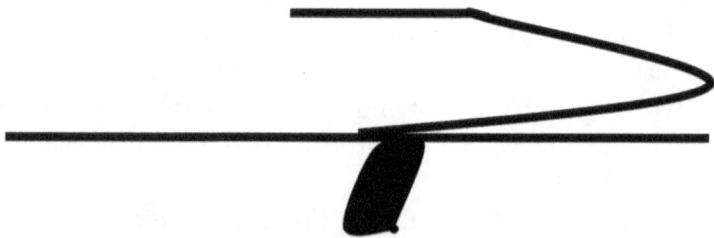

Figure 1.4. Good Shape for Fulcrum

chure that touches the reed vibrates sympathetically with the reed. The lower lip should be muscled to remove some of the harsh effect of the lower teeth.

The lips must remain muscled to allow blood to circulate, keeping the lips more sensitive. If the lower lip is nothing but a limp piece of flesh sandwiched between a hard-textured reed and hard teeth, tone quality, endurance, and flexibility will suffer. Keeping the top lip muscled will help keep the proper density of the embouchure. Think of the upper lip as being 75 percent of the embouchure, even though the upper lip does not touch the reed. The upper and lower lips work together; it is impossible to have a slack, resting upper lip and a strong, active lower lip at the same time.

Beginning students must develop the embouchure muscles over time. Most students will start on a reed strength of two, but this can vary to strength two and a half depending on the opening of the mouthpiece and the brand of the reed. The student should only practice about fifteen minutes at a time, then rest. Do not practice to the point where a proper embouchure shape cannot be maintained. Both reed strength and the length of practice time affect endurance with regard to maintaining the proper embouchure shape.

As the embouchure muscles develop, the student should move up a half reed strength and also move up in practice time. Be aware of the fact that as reeds get older, they will get softer. If the student practices on only one or two reeds for a long period of time, the tendency is that as the reed gets softer, so will the embouchure. That is why it is important to keep fresh reeds rotating in and out of your reed lineup (see chapter 2).

The *oral cavity* is probably the most sophisticated and delicate aspect of clarinet embouchure manipulation. The oral cavity is determined primarily by tongue placement and shape. The oral cavity, lip muscles, and jaw pressure must be coordinated to work together. All of the muscles necessary in forming a good clarinet embouchure usually function without conscious thought once the student has developed the correct habits. The size and shape of the oral cavity is most critical in the upper register of the clarinet. Generally, the tongue is slightly touching or just barely under the back upper molar teeth and can be moved down or up to voice notes and to help with pitch, depending upon in which register one is playing.

Note: The low register of the clarinet from written low E to third-line treble clef B-flat is the *chalumeau* register. The middle register from written middle-line B natural to C (two leger lines above treble clef) is the *clarion* register. Above this high C is the high register called the *altissimo* register. For the clarion register of the clarinet, use the oral-cavity shape and tongue position that is produced when whistling the pitch of a throat B-flat (middle line B-flat). Use this tongue position to slur in the staff.

Learn to set your altissimo embouchure when in the middle range for an upcoming altissimo passage so that the notes speak on time. Practice this by playing a high note, and then begin playing before the altissimo passage, taking care not to change the embouchure. See the end of chapter 6 for more information on tongue placement for the altissimo register.

BEGINNER

Forming the Clarinet Embouchure

1. Make the mouth round. The corners of the lips should be inward, like a round rubber band.
2. The top lip should be muscled. You should not be able to pinch the flesh under the nose; it should be tight.
3. The chin should be flat and pointed toward the ground.
4. The bottom lip should be wrinkled.
5. Only the red portion of the bottom lip touches the reed, not the flesh-colored portion. The muscle is in the red portion of the lip and only about half of this red portion folds over the teeth.
6. The bottom lip sits against the reed where the reed and the mouthpiece separate from one another.
7. The top teeth sit on the mouthpiece. The top lip does not sit between the mouthpiece and the top teeth. The mouthpiece/clarinet will enter the mouth somewhere between a 40- and 45-degree angle.
8. Use enough embouchure pressure against the reed to produce a concert C that is just slightly sharp when playing the mouthpiece and reed alone.

TEACHING TIPS

1. One should be able to form the basic embouchure before putting the mouthpiece in the mouth.
2. Most people have more success in properly shaping the lower lip if they concentrate on the upper lip muscle. Usually if the upper lip is made muscled, the lower lip and chin will form the correct shape. Try to pinch the upper lip beneath the nose. It should be firm enough so that very little flesh can be pinched. This procedure will usually flatten the chin.
3. The muscles of the lips must put pressure all around the mouthpiece and reed, much like a rubber band (not a rubber band that has been stretched flat). The lower lip should therefore be wrinkled.
4. Do not pull down on the muscles in the corners of the mouth. Likewise, do not pull up on the corners of the mouth like a smile.
5. Place just half of the red portion of the bottom lip over the teeth. Watch that the student does not allow the insertion of the mouthpiece to force more bottom lip over the teeth.
6. The cheeks must be firm and muscled. It is impossible to make a muscled embouchure unless the cheeks are also muscled enough to resist the air pressure necessary to blow the clarinet. Do not let air pockets form in the cheeks.
7. The placement of the upper teeth on the mouthpiece depends upon the angle at which the clarinet is held. For most players, this distance is three-eighths to one-half inch from the mouthpiece tip to the teeth. One way to determine this distance is to place a piece of masking tape on top of the mouthpiece. After a few minutes of playing, a slight impression is made into the tape, making it possible to measure from the mouthpiece tip to the teeth impression.

    If the student does not like to put his or her teeth on a hard mouthpiece, or has sensitive teeth, cut a mouthpiece patch out of a neoprene glove and use double-stick tape to tape it to the mouthpiece. Do not put the patch even with the tip of the mouthpiece, but place it about an eighth of an inch back from the tip. If a student has braces or rough bottom teeth, make a thin lip cushion to cover the bottom teeth out of Parafilm M, a thin plastic film. Search Parafilm M online for locations that sell this product.

(continued)

8. A technique that helps to develop the muscles in the corners of the mouth for a proper embouchure is to suck on a large straw with the end folded over and a pinhole stuck in the straw. Observe how the embouchure and cheeks pull inward. Now hold this same shape with only the facial muscles.
9. To develop embouchure muscles, place a four-inch piece of three-eighth-inch doweling rod between the lips in front of the teeth. Hold the dowel rod at less than a 90-degree angle, but do not let it drop. Do not change jaw position, but use lip muscles to support the dowel rod. See figure 1.5.

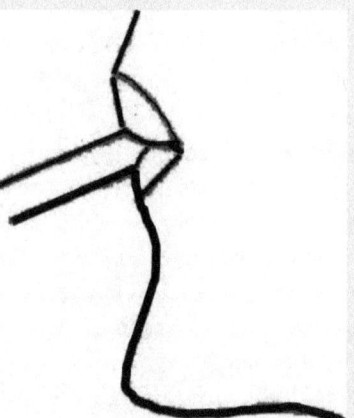

Figure 1.5. Jaw Position

10. Most teachers tell students not to move or adjust their embouchure when they play due to overadjustment. In fact, there is a slight adjustment for intonation, tone quality, adjustment for a particular register to speak on time, and so on.

    Have the student play a written low G below the staff. As the student is playing the low G, reach over and press the register key. The fourth line D (the twelfth above) should speak without any conscious embouchure change. If the D does not speak, check the amount of mouthpiece in the mouth or the amount of lower lip on the reed.

Developing a good embouchure at a young age will allow the student to progress much faster with regard to embouchure technique, that is, the ability to produce smooth interval leaps with notes speaking on time. This in turn will help improve rhythm and will help produce faster overall technique, as well as improved intonation and articulation. The time spent in developing and maintaining a good embouchure is time well spent.

NOTE

1. Roger Coppenbarger, *An Investigation of the Vibrating Clarinet Reed Utilizing High Speed Cinematography* (Unpublished dissertation, University of Missouri–Kansas City, 1970), 117, 123.

2

THE REED

Tone quality is improved when the reed functions as efficiently as possible. One can have a bad tone and play in tune, or one can have a good tone and play in tune. Between one note and the next, there is a delay or disturbance time during which the reed's vibrational speed changes. A half-step slur will create a reed disturbance time of .003 of a second, whereas an octave jump slur from open G to low G has a .057 of a second disturbance time.[1]

The reed contacts the mouthpiece with such speed that there is a slight rebound vibration in the tip. The Bernoulli Effect (which gives airplanes lift) pulls the reed to the mouthpiece.[2] The quicker the reed can establish its characteristic sound wave, the quicker the characteristic clarinet tone is established.

The stiffer the reed, the quicker it may be able to move. However, if the reed is too stiff, the air column or instrument tube and embouchure cannot control the reed, and it will want to squeak.

When a finger is changed on the clarinet, it either shortens or lengthens the clarinet, thereby making the reed vibrate faster or slower in order to vibrate in sympathy with the length of the clarinet, that is, the pitch being fingered.

A clarinet or saxophone reed only vibrates longitudinally.[3] Due to this phenomenon, it is possible to construct a reed with a heavy center spine or heart and weaker sides. A reed of this shape provides sufficient resilience to move fast, yet is soft enough to be controlled by the vibrating air column.

A poorly constructed reed will have bad tone, speak late, tongue late, and be hard to control. As you can see, it is very important to play on a good reed.

When selecting a reed, the following characteristics should be considered:

1. Cut. No bark should be on the portion of the reed that lies above the window of the mouthpiece.
2. Density. The thick end of the reed (not the tip) should show a dense configuration of cells indicating maturity. If the cells appear very porous, the reed will generally not play well. To test for density, dip the tip of the reed in water and blow hard on the butt end of the reed. Bubbles will appear on the cut portion of the reed. If the reed is easy to blow through and many bubbles appear, the cane may be too porous.
3. Color and taste. The bark of the reed should generally be a golden color and have no greenish tint. Immature cane will usually have a sour or bitter taste, while mature cane will have a neutral to slightly sweet taste.
4. Vascular bundles. If a reed is held up to a light source, fine lines called vascular bundles will be visible, especially in the tip. The vascular bundles carry water through the cane when it is alive. These vascular bundles are stronger than the surrounding material. They give the reed its *spring* and should be evenly spaced. A large gap between vascular bundles may indicate a weak spot in the reed.
5. Size. The reed should be wide enough to cover the mouthpiece side and tip rails. Any material that extends over the rails deters from the reed's efficiency and increases the chance that the reed will not seal to the mouthpiece. Since the reed closes completely to the mouthpiece, the reed must be flat on the back and seal to the mouthpiece.

THE REED

To check to see if the reed is sealing to the mouthpiece, place the bottom of the mouthpiece at the tenon, with reed attached, on a flat spot of the hand. With the mouth, suck all the air out of the mouthpiece, leaving the mouthpiece against the hand. If the reed is sealing to the mouthpiece, this will create a vacuum causing the reed to adhere to the mouthpiece for a few seconds. A nice clean pop indicates a good seal. A very *metallic* pop may indicate a reed that is too stiff. A *mushy* sounding pop or dull thud may indicate a reed that is too soft. If the reed is unable to create a seal against the mouthpiece, then the reed is not flat on the back and will have to be polished or sanded (see Break-In Process).

In rare cases, the mouthpiece may be warped. If every reed tested is unable to seal, then the problem might be in the mouthpiece, and the search for a good reed is hopeless. A repair technician can check a mouthpiece for any distortion.

6. General appearance. The tip cut should be clean and not ragged or uneven. The tip should not be wavy or warped. The reed should be symmetrical, that is, when looking at the thick end, it should not be higher on one side than on the other. The vamp or cut portion should not have gouges or be excessively rough.

BEGINNER

Preparing a New Reed

1. After selecting a new reed from the box, rub the top of the reed with your fingernail to smooth the surface where the lip will sit so the reed is not rough against the lip. Do not rub at the very tip to avoid damage to the tip.
2. Soak the new reed in water, not by licking it or holding it in your mouth, for about three minutes. Always soak reeds for at least a half minute. You can do this while you are putting your clarinet together.
3. When placing the reed on the mouthpiece, be sure there is no reed tip sitting above the mouthpiece.

(continued)

4. A ligature always tightens with the right hand as you look at the reed on the mouthpiece. Depending upon the brand of the ligature, some screws will be on the top of the mouthpiece and some will be on the reed side of the mouthpiece.

ADVANCED

The Break-in Process

The break-in process should be done before a reed is played or adjusted. The break-in takes only a few minutes and will make the reed more stable, play better, and last longer. A very smooth, slick reed is easier on the lips and will reflect the sound wave much more efficiently than one with a rough surface. The breaking-in process for a single reed consists of two basic steps:

1. Sealing the wood cells
2. Polishing the back and the vamp

Soak a new reed in water for two to three minutes; remove and allow the reed to dry on a flat glass (flat side of reed against the glass). You can use a small hand mirror for this. With the reed still on the glass, burnish the top portion of the reed (vamp) with something hard and round, such as another reed, a plastic pen cap, your fingernail, etc. The purpose is to turn the rough-cut fibers inward.

Next take a piece of #600 wet or dry emery paper and rub it against itself to knock off some of the tooth. Rub the reed lightly back and forth longitudinally with the smoothed sandpaper. This will create a little wood dust to help fill the pores. Take care to rub lightly in the tip area. You do not want to tear off pieces of the tip or to weaken the reed too much. Sealing the reed will help keep sugars and minerals from the saliva from breaking down the vascular bundles, the springs inside the reed. A properly sealed reed will last much longer in good condition.

Since the sound wave is reflected off the back of the reed while it is closed to the mouthpiece, the back of the reed must be highly polished. Place a piece of #600 emery paper on a flat glass with the rough side on the glass. Rub the back of the reed on the back side, that is, the non-rough side of the emery paper.

THE REED

To rub the reed, place three fingers on the bark portion of the reed and move the reed lengthwise. Be sure to keep the emery paper flat and taut, otherwise the reed's tip may be damaged. If there is difficulty in moving the reed, place a piece of double-stick tape on the bark of the reed to provide traction for the fingers.

After the reed has been polished, hold the reed up to the light and sight down the back of the reed. This allows light to be reflected off the back. If the reed is shiny all over, the reed is flat. Dull, unpolished spots indicate the reed is not flat. If this is true, it must be lightly sanded with #600 emery paper to flatten the back. Sand the back following the same procedure above for polishing the back, only this time sand the reed on the rough side of the emery paper. Frequently hold the reed up to the light and sight down the back of the reed. When it is shiny all over, it is flat.

The back of the reed is then once again polished on the back side of the emery paper or on typing paper. The intent here is not to soften the reed, but to flatten the back of the reed. This allows the reed to seal firmly against the mouthpiece, making it much easier to play. A reed that leaks is like a pad that leaks. It may squeak or be difficult to control. The reed is now ready to play.

TEACHING TIPS

The tip of the reed is important for high notes to speak clearly and in tune. If the tip is too soft, altissimo register notes will be difficult to play. If this is the case, try moving the reed up on the mouthpiece so that a hair's worth of reed is above the tip of the mouthpiece. Generally, the reed is placed so that a hair's worth of mouthpiece is above the tip of the reed or placed so that the reed is even with the mouthpiece.

If it is determined that the tip of the reed is too soft, use a reed clipper to clip the tip. Only clip about a typing paper's thickness of reed at a time. One can always clip more reed, but it is not possible to put the clipping back on the reed once it has been clipped. A reed that is too soft will have a tendency to play flat, whereas a reed that is too hard will have a tendency to play sharp.

New reeds should be played no more than about 15 to 20 minutes for the first few days to allow them to become conditioned to playing. Do not play high notes (above C above the staff) while the reed is being conditioned. After three or four days, the reed may be played as long as one wishes. It is suggested that a student have four to six reeds that can be rotated. Rotation allows the reeds to dry thoroughly between use, which helps them last longer; also, a student who uses only one reed will become dependent on that reed, and the student's embouchure will change as the reed deteriorates. As one reed becomes soft, it can be replaced by a new reed.

If the tip is wavy, as sometimes will be the case with new reeds, place the reed on the flat part of the mouthpiece. Place the thumb on the wavy tip, applying slight pressure. Now move the reed back and forth from side to side, not up and down. Moving the reed up and down will break the vascular bundles and make the reed soft. The intent is to *press* the wave out of the reed, much like ironing the wrinkles out of a pair of pants with an iron; however, only the heat from the thumb is used here.

If playing a low G in the chalumeau register at a soft dynamic is fuzzy, try removing (with #600 grit emery paper) a little wood about three-eighths to a quarter of an inch back from the tip, and an eighth of an inch in from either side as if sanding two eyes (see figure 2.1). This is roughly on the edge of the *heart* of the reed. The heart of the reed is an area that extends down the middle of the reed for a little over three centimeters of the roughly 35-millimeter cut portion of the reed.

The rails of the reed from the beginning cut at the back of the reed to the tip should be a gradual decline and should be the same on each side of the reed. If both sides are not symmetrical or if

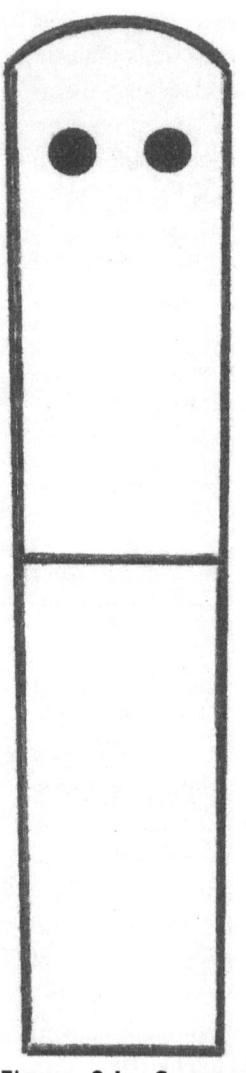

Figure 2.1. Scrape Spots to Alleviate Fuzzy Tone

there appears to be a raised spot on one side, gently sand the spot so as to create a gradual decline from the cut to the tip.

NOTES

1. Coppenbarger, *An Investigation of the Vibrating Clarinet Reed Utilizing High Speed Cinematography*, 116.
2. Coppenbarger, *An Investigation*, 119.
3. Coppenbarger, *An Investigation*, 113.

3

EQUIPMENT

CLARINET

Clarinet models change from year to year, more frequently with some manufacturers than with others, so any specific recommendations would be quickly outdated. However, the Buffet R-13 model clarinet has been the staple for clarinetists for decades. It is the model used by many orchestral clarinetists. Other good horns include the current top professional models of Yamaha, Selmer, Patricola, and Leblanc.

Most wood clarinets are made from granadilla wood (also called African black wood or Mpingo wood), due to its density. Some clarinets are made from rosewood. Although these are very nice looking, the wood is less dense and thus holds water more than granadilla wood. I have had students who, after a long rehearsal or practice, would have to let the horn dry out in order to remove the barrel due to the swelling of the wood, although my daughter has not had this problem with her rosewood clarinet. Some people do like the lighter tone produced by a rosewood clarinet.

When selecting a clarinet, listen to tone. Select a horn with a rich, dark sound. Listen for an even scale. Play a chromatic scale at a mezzo-forte level and listen for every note to speak at the same volume. If one note is muffled or difficult to play or if a note sticks out or is squawky

> **BEGINNER**
>
> Most plastic horns are of beginner level, though there are a few intermediate level clarinets made of plastic. It is recommended that a beginning elementary school student start on a plastic clarinet. Clarinets made of wood are generally more expensive and more prone to cracking due to extreme temperature changes. A high school student who has a good wooden clarinet should also have a plastic clarinet for marching band, once again due to weather issues that will stress a wooden clarinet.

sounding, pass on that horn. Pay particular attention to first line treble clef E. Sometimes this note can be stuffy feeling and will drop out in volume when compared to other notes.

Test the intonation of the clarinet. Again, play a chromatic scale and see if any notes are particularly out of tune. Watch the intonation on throat G-sharp and A (second-line and second-space treble clef). The throat tones (G through B-flat, second line through third line in treble clef) can sometimes be sharp. This will be discussed in chapter 5. Inexpensive plastic clarinets will often have sharp throat tones.

If third-line B and third-space C are fairly well in tune, then low E and F below the staff may be a little flat. This is okay. Because the clarinet overblows the interval of a twelfth, it is not possible to get both the low E and F and also B and C the twelfth above perfectly in tune. Most clarinetists play many more Bs and Cs than low Es and Fs, so most manufacturers will tend to work toward making these notes better in tune. Do not worry about keys where the springs may feel a little tight or some keys may be harder to press down than you would like; these can be adjusted by a repair technician. Inspect the horn for cracks. Refer to chapter 4 for information on where to inspect for cracks.

> **ADVANCED**
>
> Many advanced clarinetists will have a qualified repair technician replace the pads in the top section with cork pads. Cork pads will seal better and last longer than fish skin pads.

EQUIPMENT   21

Another factor to consider that is often overlooked is the quality of the case. Cases are expensive; as much as a third of the cost of a student instrument is actually the cost of the case. The case must be cushioned enough inside to keep the clarinet from moving around as you carry it, and yet not so tight of a fit (especially in the lid area) that keys may get bent.

Test the case by placing the clarinet inside, and then gently rock the case back and forth to simulate travel. Open the case to see if the clarinet has remained in its proper location. Sometimes something as simple as placing your nicely folded clarinet swab on top of the clarinet will help keep the clarinet from moving around in the case, if this is an issue. If you are buying from a shop and you like an instrument that comes with a bad case, ask if they will give you a better case.

MOUTHPIECE

There are a number of very good mouthpieces on the market today. The mouthpiece is the most critical component with regard to tone production. Prices range from an inexpensive plastic mouthpiece, suitable for a beginner who may be more prone to breaking it, to an expensive, hand-made hard rubber mouthpiece costing a few hundred dollars. For the student who has spent good money on a professional model clarinet, a good mouthpiece made of hard rubber is a must. Some clarinetists spend years looking for that *great* mouthpiece. Once they find it, they will play it for decades if it is properly maintained.

Pick a mouthpiece for tone quality and tonguing ability. Care must be taken not to pick the *reed* one is using, but to pick the mouthpiece. Therefore, try several different reeds of several brands on the mouthpiece and look for consistency in the tone and the ability to tongue the mouthpiece. Also be aware that if you change to a different clarinet, that mouthpiece may not fit the new clarinet. But, if you have a mouthpiece that you love, pick a new clarinet that will fit that mouthpiece.

Most plastic clarinets come with inexpensive plastic mouthpieces. The student's tone will be greatly improved on a plastic clarinet if a low-end hard rubber mouthpiece is purchased. As the student matures and moves to a wooden clarinet, the student will probably want to also move up in quality of mouthpiece. Mouthpiece quality pretty much follows price range; that is, the more expensive, generally the better.

The length of the lay of the mouthpiece and of course the length of the mouthpiece itself affect pitch.

LIGATURE

The function of the ligature is to hold the reed to the mouthpiece so that the reed seals and does not leak. Although this would seem like a simple task, thus limiting the selection of ligatures, this is not the case. There are dozens and dozens of ligatures on the market. They vary from an inexpensive piece of Velcro to those selling for well over $100 retail price. Beware of some cheap metal ligatures that will squeeze the reed on the sides, causing the reed to rise in the center and thus leak. The ligature should pull the reed to the mouthpiece by applying even pressure over the entire reed. The ligature will have an effect upon tone quality and the ability to tongue.

Many clarinetists like the Rovner ligature, available in a number of different models. This ligature is made from a soft material that absorbs some of the vibrations from the mouthpiece and thus many believe produces a darker sound. A metal ligature, in general, produces a slightly brighter sound. However, a metal ligature is sometimes easier to tongue than a soft ligature. Having said this, you may wish to use a different

---

TEACHING TIP

Some ligatures will tighten with the screws sitting on the reed side of the mouthpiece and some will tighten with the ligature screws on the top side of the mouthpiece. When in doubt, be aware that all ligatures tighten with the screws on the right side. That is, as one looks at the reed, the ligature will tighten with the right hand. If the ligature looks as if it tightens with the left hand, then the ligature is backward. There are no left-hand-tightening ligatures. Whether the ligature tightens with the screws on the bottom (reed side) of the mouthpiece or the top side of the mouthpiece depends upon the design of the ligature.

EQUIPMENT

> **TEACHING TIP**
>
> Tighten the ligature just tight enough to hold the reed in place. The ligature should not leave a dent or mark on the reed. If this is the case, you are tightening the ligature too tight. In some ligatures, over tightening will have the effect of choking off the reed since the entire reed actually vibrates. This may have an effect on tone. If the reed is not flat on the back and not sealing to the mouthpiece, no amount of tightening will make the reed seal to the mouthpiece. If this is the case, the back of the reed will need to be flattened (see chapter 2).

ligature for different situations. One would be more inclined to use a metal ligature for Dixieland music or in band, but a soft ligature for a concerto or sonata, in orchestra, or for chamber music.

REED

Years ago there were just a few brands of reeds from which to choose. Today there are many brands, all competing for your business. There is no industry standard with regard to strength, but as a rule, most brands are rather close to one another with regard to strength. A beginning clarinetist is probably going to start on strength number two. As the embouchure matures, he or she should move up to strength number two and a half.

If beginning in fifth grade, by the time he or she is in seventh grade, the student will probably be playing on strength number three. From about ninth or tenth grade through high school, the student will probably be playing strength three and a half. This is assuming students practice regularly and increase in embouchure strength as they mature. A student who takes some time off practicing during vacations will have to play on older or softer reeds while rebuilding his or her embouchure.

Some brands of reeds may work better on some mouthpieces or clarinets or work better for some players than other brands. Try several different brands of reeds. Once you find a brand and strength that you like, it is best to stay with it, unless something new comes on the market that you just have to try.

Some clarinetists prefer to buy reeds that are a half strength stiffer than they plan to use in order to have a little extra wood available to allow for polishing or sanding the reed (see chapter 2). You may find some reeds easier to tongue than others, or some will have a darker sound; some will have both good qualities and poorer qualities. It is part of your job as a clarinetist to find and maintain reeds that work with your particular equipment, and your particular embouchure and oral cavity.

BARREL

The barrel is actually an extension of the mouthpiece. Many clarinetists will look for that great barrel just the same as they look for that great mouthpiece. It is important that the barrel fit both the mouthpiece and the clarinet. The standard barrel is sixty-six millimeters in length, but it is advisable to have a shorter and longer barrel available for intonation purposes (see chapter 5).

The barrel is also selected for tone quality, the ability to tongue, and the ease at which intervals change—the same criteria one uses when selecting a mouthpiece. The barrel may be made of a synthetic material or made from any number of varieties of wood. Beginners should use the barrel that comes with the instrument, unless it is damaged, chipped, or cracked.

4

MAINTENANCE

The clarinet, like any musical instrument, must be maintained in proper working condition. If a student experiences persistent problems with response, intonation, squeaking, or particular notes not sounding, a few minutes spent checking the instrument will save hours of frustrating and fruitless practice. Students should learn how to handle, maintain, and clean the instrument correctly in order to minimize damage to the mechanism.

Apply cork grease to the cork tenons of the joints as often as is necessary to allow for easy assembly. Take care during assembly not to bend or place excessive pressure on the keys. Pay particular attention to the side keys and pinky keys that the student does not bend these keys when putting the clarinet together. Sometimes a student may have learned to put the horn together properly, but may become inattentive over time. Be sure to press the rings on the top section down to lift the lever that connects the top section to the bottom section so that the cork on the connecting rod is not torn off.

The clarinet should be swabbed two or three times after each use. Wooden instruments need to be swabbed to prevent moisture from causing the wood to swell or crack, and even plastic clarinets need to be swabbed to stay clean. Remove the mouthpiece before swabbing. Use a swab made of cloth, not chamois. Chamois does not absorb moisture well and may become hard and stiff over time, possibly scratching the bore of the instrument. A swab made of silk or a cotton blend is best. Some swabs made entirely of cotton may leave cotton residue in tone holes over a long period of time.

The mouthpiece must be kept clean. Remove the reed and ligature each time you disassemble the clarinet and then wipe the mouthpiece out from the inside with the swab wrapped around your finger. If you pull the swab across the tip, you will gradually wear down the tip and thus change the mouthpiece. Periodically clean the mouthpiece with lukewarm water and lemon juice. The lemon juice will act as a mild acid, but will not harm the rubber in the mouthpiece or leave an unpleasant taste, as some soaps or detergents may.

Always store the mouthpiece in a mouthpiece cap to protect the tip. A chip in the tip of a mouthpiece will cause the clarinet to squeak, and in some cases not to make a sound at all, because the reed will be unable to seal against the chipped area.

Clean tone holes about once per month using a dry cotton swab. The keys, or rather the screws holding the keys in place, should be oiled two or three times per year with key oil, which you may purchase at your local music store. For this procedure, back a screw partway out of the post and place a drop of oil on the screw rod, then screw it back in place.

The clarinet pads must have an airtight seal so that the clarinet acoustically functions properly. If a pad leaks, the clarinet will be difficult to play and could possibly squeak. To check for a leaking pad, remove one

BEGINNER

Swab the clarinet by dropping the swab into the bell end of the clarinet. This will allow the swab to extend before it reaches the register pipe and therefore will be less likely to become stuck. Always remove the reed from the mouthpiece when putting the instrument away. If the reed stays on the mouthpiece, mold may develop. The reed will also have a tendency to shape itself to the mouthpiece's curvature and become soft quicker. Also, you should be rotating your reeds, which means you should play on a different one next time.

MAINTENANCE

section of the clarinet. Cover all the tone holes/keys, as if fingering a middle C when checking the upper section, or right-hand low E when checking the lower section. Now place the open end of the section against the palm of the hand and blow into the other end. There should be some resistance against the air pressure. Listen for leaking air. If a pad is found to be leaking, it must be replaced.

Sometimes a pad may leak due to a bent key. A warble sound when playing a low E may be caused by the Ab/Eb key blowing open due to a weak spring. Sometimes the leak is caused not by a poorly sealing pad but by a crack in the instrument itself. If a crack is found in the clarinet, an experienced repair technician must repair it. Cracks are most often found around the register pipe and the throat "A" tone hole.

Sometimes it may be necessary to make an emergency repair. A small toolkit may be useful for such quick repairs. Periodically check for loose screws. If a screw continues to loosen, you can tighten the loose screw with a piece of sewing thread inserted into the metal threads. Any thread sticking out can be cut or burned off. A loose-fitting joint can be wrapped with paper or if the cork is totally missing, some electrical tape or waxed dental floss can be wrapped around the tenon. This is a temporary fix, and the clarinet should be taken to a repair technician to replace the missing or damaged cork.

A broken spring may possibly be replaced temporarily with a rubber band, if it is a key that is normally closed (for example the C#/G# key). In an emergency situation, a missing screw may be replaced with a round toothpick. These repairs are temporary; a qualified technician should repair the instrument as soon as possible.

TEACHING TIP

Wood clarinets crack most often during dry winter months. Therefore, to keep a wood clarinet from cracking, place a small moist sponge in the case, taking care not to let the sponge touch the clarinet. Some students prefer to use orange peel, as this will add a nice bouquet to the case. When the orange peel dries out, it is time to replace it. If the orange peel starts to mold, then there is enough moisture in the case and you no longer need to add moisture. The violin-sized Dampit also works for this.

If a pad falls out of a pad cup, there may be enough glue left in the cup to replace the pad without having to remove the key. Heat the cup, preferably with a soldering iron rather than an open flame, and slip the pad in. If using heat on a plastic clarinet, be careful not to melt a tone hole. For a sticky pad, pull a dollar bill under the pad.

It may be of value to learn to replace a torn tenon cork, as this is a very common problem with student instruments. With a little practice, this is not a difficult procedure and a skill that will come in quite handy. If you make a mistake, no big deal; it was going to the shop for a cork replacement anyway. You will need a sheet of cork. Most often one-eighth-inch thickness will work. You will also need contact cement to glue it on to the clarinet tenon. Only use contact cement, not any other kind of glue. A file, such as a fingernail file, may be used to fit the cork joint to the tenon.

First make a template from an existing clarinet by wrapping a piece of paper around the tenon. Take care to account for width. Be sure to label it as *upper top joint*, *lower top joint*, or *bottom joint*, depending upon which joint the template is made from, as the same template cannot be used for all the cork joints because they are of different sizes. Be sure to use as a template a clarinet that has the cork on the joint. If a template is made from a joint with no cork on it, it will be too small. Add just a little extra length to the template to account for different thicknesses of cork or minor variations in clarinet thickness.

Lay the template on a sheet of one-eighth-inch-thick cork. Try to cut the length with the grain as it will be easier to cut than cross grain. You may want to use a razor blade to cut the cork.

Bevel the edge of the cork. This is the edge that the cork will wrap across. Do not try to butt the ends together, as you may be off due to the thickness of contact cement that will be used to glue the cork onto the joint. See figure 4.1.

Hit the piece of flat cork all over with a hammer to help make it pliable. Be sure to thoroughly clean the old cork from the clarinet joint. Place contact cement on the grooved part of the clarinet tenon. Place

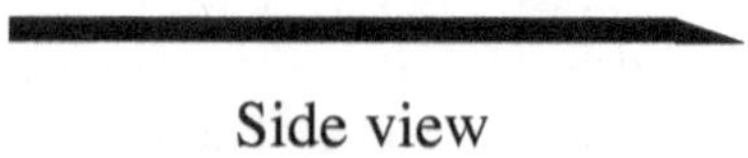

Side view

Figure 4.1. Side View Bevel Edge of Cork

MAINTENANCE

contact cement on the slanted beveled edge (*but not on the top*) and the *back* of the cork. The back is the portion that will lie against the grooved portion of the tenon. Let the contact cement dry until it is tacky, not sticky (about twenty minutes).

Contact cement only sticks to itself, which is why contact cement must be placed on both the cork and the tenon joint. After both the cork and tenon are tacky, carefully wrap the cork around the tenon. Note that the contact cement will instantly adhere to itself and cannot be repositioned after it touches itself.

Apply pressure to the cork to remove any air bubbles between the cork and tenon joint. The contact cement will strengthen the cork, so it should not tear as you wrap it around the tenon. Overlap the cork just to the point where cement touches cement. You may need to use a razor blade to cut off any extra length of cork. Wrap the cork with yarn or parachute cord to hold it in place while it dries overnight. If wrapping with string be careful not to cut grooves in the cork.

After the cement is thoroughly dry, take the fingernail file and sand a slight angle to the bottom edge of the cork where the joint is going to receive the bell, bottom joint or barrel. This is so the two joints go together easier and the cork does not tear; see figure 4.2.

Apply plenty of cork grease and test to see if the joints go together easily. If they are too tight, wipe off the cork grease and evenly sand the joint with the fingernail file. Be aware that you can always sand more cork off, but you cannot put it back on. Therefore, sand and test to see if the joints fit often.

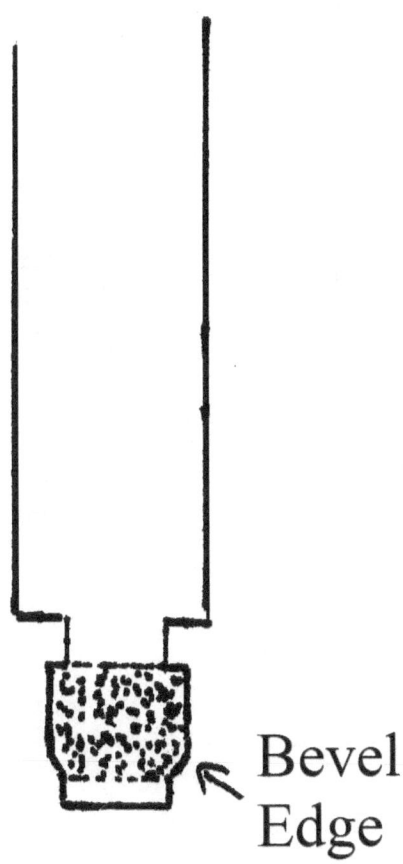

Figure 4.2. Cork Joint

> **TEACHING TIP**
>
> The instrument case is often overlooked when it comes to clarinet maintenance. A horn that is continually found to have bent keys may be due to a worn out padding inside the instrument case. If the student puts music books on top of the horn inside the case, this may also cause bent keys. Music books should be carried in the case cover, if there is one, or in a separate bag. A soft thin cloth laid over the clarinet might be sufficient to keep it from moving inside the case.

Avoid using alcohol as a cleaner on plastic clarinets as this may cause some plastics to become brittle. Sometimes a plastic horn can shrink in the cold. I have a plastic bass clarinet where the keys (not pads) will stick or bind in the right hand when it first comes in from the cold. Once the horn has warmed up to room temperature, the keys stopped binding. One would not think that plastic will shrink from cold temperature, but it can.

The following clarinet inspection sheet may be copied and used to help with the band program's instrument inventory. It may also be used for individual students to notify parents as to what may need attention with regard to the student's clarinet. The band director may want to modify this sheet to be used with other instruments.

> **INSTRUMENT INSPECTION CHECKLIST FOR CLARINET**
>
> *Cross out number if checked okay, circle number if needs attention*
>
> **Mouthpiece**
>   1. Check for chip in tip or side rails
>   2. Needs cleaning
>   3. Tenon cork needs replacing
>
> **Upper Section**
>   1. Check for cracks or chipped tone holes
>   2. Tenon corks needs replacing

MAINTENANCE

3. Chip in tenon
4. Tone holes need cleaning
5. Bent keys, list _____
6. Missing screws, list _____
7. Missing key corks, list keys _____
8. Screws need oiling
9. Pads need replacing, circle: Register key, Throat A, Throat G#, Top side, 2nd side, 3rd Side, Side Eb/Bb, Pinky C#/G#, Sliver Eb/Bb, Top ring pad, 2nd ring pad

Lower Section

1. Connecting lever between upper and lower section missing cork, needs adjusting
2. Check for cracks or chipped tone holes
3. Tenon cork needs replacing
4. Chip in tenon or receiver
5. Tone holes need cleaning
6. Bent keys, list _____
7. Missing screws, list _____
8. Missing key corks, list keys _____
9. Screws need oiling
10. Crow foot (Right hand F#/C#, E/B) needs adjusting
11. Right hand top pinky Ab/Eb, F/C needs adjusting
12. Left hand alternate F/C, E/B, F#/C# needs adjusting
13. Pads need replacing, circle: 1st ring pad, B/F# Sliver, Ab/Eb pad, F/C pad, F#/C# pad, E/B pad

Barrel and Bell

1. Check for cracks

Case

1. Handle, locks need repair
2. Check for wear inside case

5

INTONATION

One of the many concerns of the band director is the continuing effort to keep the clarinet section in tune. Because the clarinet overblows the interval of a twelfth rather than an octave like the rest of the woodwinds, there are some inherent pitch problems to frustrate the band director as well as the student. A number of elements go into tuning the clarinet section of a band. Some basics are necessary in order for a clarinetist to play in tune.

The clarinet is designed to be in tune at 72 degrees Fahrenheit when the barrel is pulled about one millimeter, using a medium-to-medium-hard reed and a correct embouchure. Most clarinets use a barrel that is 66 millimeters in length. A synthetic barrel, that is, a hard rubber barrel made of the same material as the mouthpiece, is less prone to change due to condensation than a wooden barrel. This is the reason clarinet mouthpieces are no longer made of wood. Some clarinetists, therefore, believe a synthetic barrel makes for more stable intonation.

There are a number of makers of synthetic barrels of this type that a clarinetist may wish to try. This is not to say that a wooden barrel is bad. There are a number of wooden barrels available, made of a variety of different woods. Some clarinetists believe that different types of wood produce a variation in tone. If you like the tone of a wooden barrel and

> **BEGINNER**
>
> One should warm up by playing low notes (using the entire length of the clarinet) for about three to five minutes before tuning. When the clarinet is first removed from the case, it may be cool and take a few minutes to warm up to room temperature. A cold horn will be flat.

it plays in tune, by all means, play that barrel. However, do not be afraid or hesitant to retune during rehearsal should the intonation change as the barrel warms up or absorbs moisture.

A proper embouchure is necessary for good intonation and good tone. A poor tone is difficult to tune because it is acoustically unstable. Pulling out or pushing in to adjust the pitch is no substitute for correct embouchure placement and form, because the incorrect embouchure will cause a variety of problems beyond basic pitch. The lower lip of the embouchure must sit where the reed parts from the mouthpiece, which is about three-eighths of an inch from the mouthpiece tip. This is necessary for a proper *fulcrum*; that is, a proper balance on the embouchure where the reed is neither choked off nor difficult to control.

If too little mouthpiece is in the mouth, the tone will be thin, muffled, and the pitch will have a tendency to be flat. If too much mouthpiece is in the mouth, the tone will be shrill, the pitch may be flat, and the reed will be difficult to control and may want to squeak. Of great importance is the use of proper embouchure pressure. The amount of pressure required to play the clarinet in tune is the same pressure required to play the mouthpiece and reed alone at the pitch of concert C that is about ten cents sharp.

If too much pressure is used, the student will tend to play sharp. If the embouchure pressure is too loose, the student will play flat. If the student has too much lip on the reed, that is, if the reed is sitting on the flesh-colored part of the lip, which has little muscle, the pitch will be flat due to a weak embouchure. Do not pocket air in the cheeks as this can distort tone and pitch.

Quite often after playing for a while, younger students' embouchures will tire and this is when pitch problems start to arise. The band director should encourage students to check their embouchure when the pitch goes bad, rather than automatically assuming it is the clarinet and pulling out or pushing in to compensate.

INTONATION

It may be necessary to rest younger bands after playing for a while by speaking about rhythms, dynamics, or some musical aspect of a particular piece. They can maintain musical focus by clapping through difficult rhythms or singing melodies. The band director must remain sensitive to issues of fatigue, especially with younger players. They will not continue in band if it causes them pain and frustration.

Proper breath support is essential. Tone can be improved if one thinks of blowing *faster* air through the clarinet. The clarinetist should blow a cold, focused air stream and not a warm, wide air stream, such as a saxophonist does.

When playing loud, the student must be sure to blow harder to get louder and not loosen the embouchure to get louder. Loosening the

---

TEACHING TIP

The clarinetist should generally play with 12–15 ounces of air pressure. To measure air pressure, find an air pressure gauge that measures in ounces per square inch and not pounds per square inch. The company Marsh Bellofram makes one that is about two and a half inches in diameter that measures from 0 to 30 ounces per square inch. The part number is G24501. You will have to find a distributor that can order it for you from the company.

To the nib on the bottom of the gauge, attach a rubber hose with an inside diameter of three-eighths of an inch. To this hose attach a one-eighth-inch hose by a connector that you can find in the plumbing supply area. You may have to tie the hoses on by the use of oboe reed string. If you have difficulty getting the end of the hose over the nib, try dipping one end of the hose in boiling water for a minute to soften it, then use needle-nose pliers placed inside the hose to open the hose wider. This may be a two-person operation; one person holds the hose open, and the other inserts the nib.

In the end of the smallest hose, insert a small plastic coffee stirrer type of straw. As the student blows a note at the forte level, insert the straw in the corner of the student's mouth, trying not to disturb the embouchure. If the student has a thin sound, he or she is probably blowing less than ten ounces of air pressure and needs to blow more air through the horn. In other words, the student needs more breath support. Be sure to discard the straw and insert a clean one for the next student.

embouchure will cause the pitch to go flat. The clarinet has a tendency to go sharp when playing at soft dynamic levels. During the course of a diminuendo, the pitch will tend to go sharp, and likewise during a crescendo, the pitch will tend to go flat. If the student is playing on too soft a reed, the pitch will usually be flat. Conversely, if the reed is too stiff, the pitch will want to go sharp.

On many clarinets, third space C is usually a little sharp. This is in order to bring up the pitch of low F that is the twelfth below. Throat A (second space treble clef) tends to be sharp on many less expensive clarinets. Sometimes it is possible to put the right hand down to lower the pitch slightly when playing a throat A. It is also possible to lower the pitch of throat A by removing the A key and placing a very small piece of electrical tape in the top of the tone hole, taking up only about one-third of the space of the tone hole. The idea is not to fill in the tone hole, but rather to move the tone hole about a millimeter down on the clarinet.

Some students with a good reed will overcompensate for high notes (above high C) and pinch in the altissimo register, causing the pitch to be sharp, while others, with a poor reed or weak embouchure, will play flat in the altissimo register. Some students will move or drop their jaw when tonguing, causing the pitch to go flat.

After warming up the band, the clarinet section should tune to a fifth line written F. This tunes the middle of the clarinet. Tuning to third space C (concert B-flat) is difficult since many clarinets tend to play C on the sharp side (as mentioned earlier). Therefore, if the C is perfectly in tune, some of the right-hand low notes will tend to be flat. Open G should also be tuned in order to tune the throat tones and determine proper barrel length. If sharp, pull out at the barrel; never pull at the mouthpiece. Many students pull at the middle joint, but this causes problems with the connecting bar that allows for one & one E-flat/B-flat fingering.

Pulling at the bell only affects the last three or four notes on the clarinet, since a note generally speaks at the first available opening. You can see this by playing a note in the left hand (with a tuner), then remove the bell. There is no pitch change; therefore, the note speaks prior to reaching the bell. If one must pull more than a couple millimeters, tuning rings must be used to keep the throat tones in tune. Tuning rings are thin plastic or metal washer-like rings that fill in the gap between the barrel and upper joint. Tuning rings may be purchased at your local music store, or online if not available locally.

INTONATION

If a clarinet, especially a plastic clarinet, continually plays flat after taking into account all the above procedures, the socket at a joint may be too long. With a dial micrometer, measure the tenon and the receiving socket. If the socket is longer that the tenon, there is a gap between sections.

If the gap is between the barrel and top joint, gently sand the barrel using 600 grit emery paper to reduce the gap. Sand just a little at a time, measuring as you sand, as the gap may be a millimeter or less. If there is a gap between the tenon and socket, but the clarinet is in tune, using a tuning ring to fill in the gap will not affect the pitch, but may make some interval jumps easier to speak. Remember, however, if the clarinet is sharp and you must pull more than a couple millimeters, you must use a tuning ring to keep the throat tones in tune.

If there is a gap between the tenon and socket in the middle joint, use a tuning ring of the correct size to fill in the gap to help the clarinet speak better. Remember, the clarinet should not appear any different after adding the tuning ring; you are simply filling in an existing gap between the tenon and socket. If the gap is a millimeter or more, you will have to take some of the side keys off in order to sand the receiver of the middle joint. An experienced woodwind repair technician best does this procedure.

A gap between the lower joint and the bell is of little significance, because so few notes are affected.

If there is a gap between the barrel and mouthpiece, it is best to leave it alone. A mouthpiece change later on by the student may reduce this gap. Only sand a tenon on the clarinet if you know what you are doing! It is best to have an experienced repair person do this type of work.

Before having work done on the tenons, if a clarinet is flat, you may want to try a 64- or 65-millimeter barrel. This may be an easy fix to horns that play flat, assuming the embouchure and reeds are not the problem, as mentioned above. A recent purchase of a first-line rosewood clarinet for my daughter found the need to use a 64-millimeter barrel rather than the standard 66 millimeters due to the fact that the bell was a couple millimeters longer than the standard bell, making the overall length of the clarinet a couple millimeters longer. Of course this was taken into account in the bore size of the clarinet. Just a millimeter or two will make a big difference in intonation.

A music store employee once said that some of the inexpensive plastic clarinets were being produced with 64- or 65-millimeter barrels rather than the standard 66 millimeters to compensate for poor student embouchures, which have a tendency to play flat. There is no way to know how consistent this is in the industry or even if it is true, but for any intonation problems that appear to be horn related, first measure the barrel to determine its length and make adjustments in the barrel.

Some clarinetists will carry different sizes of barrels to compensate for changes in temperature. If performing in an air-conditioned auditorium causes the clarinet to be flat due to the cold temperature and you cannot push the barrel in any further, you may have to put on a shorter barrel. If performing outside in a community band during the hot summer months, you may have to put on a longer barrel if sharp.

My students keep both a practice and intonation chart. The practice chart helps to remind students to practice and gives them a visual progress report (see table 5.1). The intonation chart helps students keep track of possible problematic notes on their particular horn. Each note, or notes within the student's range, is plotted in a box. If the note is in tune, the student puts a zero in both the sharp box and the flat box under that particular pitch (see tables 5.2, 5.3, 5.4). If the note is sharp, the student writes in how many cents sharp the note is in the sharp box under the note, or if flat, in the flat box.

In this manner, students can plot intonation trends on their horn. If a note is always sharp or always flat, the student can learn to adjust for

Table 5.1. Practice Record

Wk/Day	1	2	3	4	5	6	7	8	9	10	11	12	13	14	15
Mon															
Tues															
Wed															
Thurs															
Fri															
Sat															
Sun															
Total Hours															

Table 5.2. Intonation Chart Octave 1

Octave 1	Pitch	E	F	F#/Gb	G	G#/Ab	A	A#/Bb	B	C	C#/Db	D	D#/Eb
	Sharp												
	Flat												

Table 5.3. Intonation Chart Octave 2

Octave 2	Pitch	E	F	F#/Gb	G	G#/Ab	A	A#/Bb	B	C	C#/Db	D	D#/Eb
	Sharp												
	Flat												

Table 5.4. Intonation Chart Octave 3

Octave 3	Pitch	E	F	F#/Gb	G	G#/Ab	A	A#/Bb	B	C	C#/Db	D	D#/Eb
	Sharp												
	Flat												

Table 5.5. Practicing Self-Assessment

Area ▶ Value ▼	Tone	Intonation	Rhythm	Musicality (Dynamics, Phrasing, etc.)	Articulation	Technique
5 - 5.5 Excellent (consistent, quality)						
4 - 4.5 Good (Mostly consistent, minor errors)						
3 - 3.5 Average (Inconsistent, errors detract from playing)						
2 - 2.5 Below Ave. (Unaware, limited ability)						
1 - 1.5 Needs Improving (Lacks ability, many errors)						

that note. This also helps to train the student's ear, and helps then to start thinking about intonation.

It is suggested that the band director develop a practice self-assessment rubric, similar to the example in table 5.5. This will get the student thinking about the different areas listed and allow for a qualitative analysis of each. This can be given at the beginning, middle, and end of the semester. Perhaps the greatest benefit of music class is that the student learns self-control and self-awareness.

A tool such as this rubric gives both the student and the band director a framework for this type of learning. It also lets the band director know how the student is thinking. If the student evaluates him- or herself as excellent in an area, but the band director evaluates the student as below average, then perhaps there needs to be some time spent with the student as to course expectations.

Although many factors are involved in tuning the clarinet section, if students use a proper embouchure and continually strive for a good tone, intonation will improve. With improved intonation, ensemble playing will be a more enjoyable experience for the students, the director, and the audience.

6

ARTICULATION

Tongue position when tonguing the clarinet reed is difficult to discuss because one cannot see the tongue while playing, and the tongue is somewhat of an involuntary muscle. The complex movements necessary while chewing food and talking are accomplished without any or much thought. It is not uncommon for a student to be unaware of the position and behavior of the tongue while playing a musical instrument. The problem is complicated by the fact that there is a great variety in size, shape, and length of each individual's tongue as well as in the oral cavity that encloses the tongue. However, every person who has sufficient control to speak normally can also learn correct articulation.

Generally, the back of the tongue sits just below or just touches the bottom of the top back molar teeth. The tongue should be approximately in the same position as when one whistles a concert Bb above middle C. It may be helpful to think of blowing cold air or a narrow air stream, about the size of a pencil eraser. As the clarinetist's range extends into the altissimo register, one may find that the back of the tongue may need to be positioned differently to allow the high notes to speak. The lowest notes on the clarinet may require the tongue to be low in the mouth, as if saying *ah*.

With regard as to which part of the tongue touches the reed, this subject is more difficult to address, primarily due to different tongue lengths and different concepts of where the *tip* of the tongue begins. Since the front of the tongue is rounded, the point on the tongue that an individual may consider to be the tip may vary by a few millimeters from one person to the next. However, a movement of just a few millimeters may make a great deal of difference when discussing contact points on the tongue.

The first thing one must remember when tonguing is that the tongue is a muscle and as such it should be used to its greatest advantage. The tongue must have shape; that is, it must be muscled. The tongue should be thought of as having an arched shape from side to side, rather than being flat. This gives the feeling of the tongue having a *spine*. A properly shaped embouchure helps produce a properly shaped tongue. The shape of the tongue lengthwise, front to back, is somewhat predetermined by tongue length as well as the size and shape of the oral cavity.

When tonguing, think of using the center of the tongue approximately an eighth of an inch behind the tip or end of the tongue, contacting a point in the center of the reed just below the edge of the tip of the reed. Only move about the first half inch of the end of the tongue when tonguing. Do not move the entire tongue in the mouth, as this will tend to alter the pitch by altering the shape and volume of the oral cavity. Also, a larger motion takes more time to accomplish; if the tongue moves any farther than absolutely necessary, the tonguing will be slower and the student will be unable to articulate at high speeds.

You should not see movement in the neck or dropping of the jaw when tonguing. Movement in this area detracts from the efficiency of tongue movement, affecting not only articulation but also pitch and tone.

Use the same contact point as you would if saying the syllable *Tu*. A French *Teu* sound is good for normal tonguing because it helps keep the embouchure round. Notice that there are several versions of the consonant *T* depending on whether the tongue is arched or cupped. A more cupped *T* is wetter, closer to an *S*, whereas a more arched *T* is harder and is closer to a *D*. The arched *T* is preferable, partly because it involves less tongue motion and therefore creates a faster articulation. This tongue position will be used for *normal* tonguing passages.

Some students might find it easier to think of a Du rather than a Tu sound; a student should be encouraged to try a variety of approaches until he or she finds the basic tongue position that allows an easy, fast articulation.

> **ADVANCED**
>
> The student should be able to tongue the reed with different degrees of pressure and contact points as in Dee, Tee, and Lee, for example. These may vary with regard to type of articulation; legato, staccato, and so on. Like string players, wind players should have an expressive vocabulary of articulations.

Beginning students will frequently play each articulated note separately, stopping the air between notes and sometimes even taking a new breath between each note. It helps them to think of polysyllabic words such as *potato*. This encourages the student to realize that the notes are connected even though they are articulated.

Another method is to have the student blow a long tone, telling the student to quickly touch the reed with the tongue and then quickly remove it, continuing the long tone every time the teacher snaps his or her fingers. It is best to hide your fingers behind the student's head so the student is not concentrating on your fingers, but rather listening for the snap. Most students will listen intently for the sound of the snap and will then tongue the reed without much thought, almost like a reflex action. In this manner, the student is less likely to move the jaw or neck or use too much tongue on the reed. There simply is not enough time to overthink the tonguing process.

The clarinetist should be able to use a variety of articulations. For example, a staccato similar to a violin staccato with the bow back and forth on the string produces a drier type of staccato. A staccato such as a violin *spiccato* where the bow bounces off the string produces a more resonant staccato. The clarinetist can achieve this type of staccato by adding a little breath push along with the staccato tongue action. Tongue placement and shape within the aural cavity is also important when producing a staccato articulation with resonance.

Also for staccato passages, try tonguing closer to the tip of the reed, the tip of the tongue, or both. Students often play staccato notes too heavily, which severely limits the possible speed. An intermediate student should be able to tongue sixteenth notes at a tempo of 120 for the quarter note.

> **TEACHING TIP**
>
> Do not accent staccato notes (unless marked); simply keep them short and light.

Think of tonguing on top of the air-column, and not through the air-column. It is as if one were to drink something that is hot. You want to lightly, and just barely, touch the hot liquid until you know how hot it is. You do not stick your tongue all the way down into the liquid. The same tone used in slow passages is used for staccato passages. Often the student focuses more time on getting the notes short and forgets the importance of always playing with a nice sound.

For legato-tongued passages, one may wish to slightly change the contact points on the reed, tongue, or both—possibly moving away from the tip of the reed and/or tongue, while at the same time tonguing with less force. A good technique is to stand to practice legato. Standing allows for a more open airway. Sitting for a long period tends to lead to poor posture, especially in the lower back, which collapses the rib cage and lungs and does not allow for a smooth, controlled air stream required for legato playing.

Be aware that the fingers should contact the tone holes squarely without making a popping sound. When playing a legato interval involving two or more fingers, squeeze and release the fingers in one fluid action. Pay particular attention when two hands are involved. Because there is no gap between legato notes, the tiniest irregularity of fingering will be audible. Students should practice scales and arpeggios slurred as well as tongued to focus on smooth transitions between notes.

Another type of articulation to take into account is how to start a note. In most cases, the tongue and air begin at the same time when starting a note. However, there may be times when the clarinetist may wish to place the tongue on the reed and build up the air pressure, then take the tongue off the reed producing a quicker start and a slight accent to the note. Style, musicality, and the type of articulation called for will help to determine how to begin a note.

Moving the tongue-reed contact points by just a millimeter may seem like a drastic change. Keep in mind that the tongue acts like a valve that opens and closes, allowing air to vibrate the reed. Do not stop blowing

ARTICULATION

> **BEGINNER**
>
> Pay particular attention not to chew with the embouchure to simulate tonguing. The tongue must touch the reed when the player articulates.

or back off on air pressure between notes. Keep air pressure constant and consistent against the reed.

Remember that the tongue must actually touch the reed for a fraction of a second to stop the reed from vibrating, thus the term *tonguing*. Some beginners will back away from the sensation of touching the reed with the tongue, and will create all their articulations in the back of the tongue, articulating Ku instead of Tu or Du. This, of course, makes it impossible for them to develop any speed; it also creates tension in the neck and jaw, and narrows the oral cavity, harming the pitch and tone.

Practice tonguing with just the mouthpiece and barrel in front of a tuner. Make sure the pitch does not go flat as you tongue. If the pitch goes more than about five cents flat, you may be moving your jaw as you tongue.

Without getting into the technique of traditional double tonguing, there is a simple form of double tonguing proposed by an early flute teacher by the name of Johann Joachim Quantz (1697–1773). I have taken this technique and developed it for use on clarinet.

Use the syllable Tee in the tip of the tongue, contacting a point a little behind the tip of the reed. Then use the syllable Dee, which is a very little bit further back on the tongue but more on the tip of the reed. Now go Tee-Tee-Dee-Dee; Tee-Tee-Dee-Dee. Try to get the very slightest rocking-like motion in the tongue contacting two points on the reed that are almost in the same spot. Practice for even notes as well as speed, and listen carefully to the pitch to ensure there is no fluctuation between the two articulations.

DEVELOPING A FOCUSED TONE WHILE TONGUING

Quite often, a student's tone will suffer during tongued passages because the student is concentrating on the act of tonguing and not on tone quality. To develop a focused tone while tonguing, try the following procedure.

1. Prepare to play by forming a good embouchure. Be sure that the top lip sitting on the mouthpiece has a clean line. If you have a natural point to your lip, slightly roll the outer edge of the lip under to create a clean line, but do not use a double lip embouchure (that is, do not put your top lip between the teeth and the mouthpiece, the upper teeth should sit on the mouthpiece). Take a proper breath, building up air pressure *while* the tongue is against the reed. Take the tongue off the reed, allowing the note to sound. Stop blowing. Rest for a couple seconds and repeat. (See figure 6.1.) This slow practice is the essential foundation of fast technique.

Figure 6.1. Starting Note with Tongue against Reed

2. Play the first note as in step one, however, this time do not stop blowing between notes. Place the tongue against the reed while continuing to keep the air pressure against the reed. Release the tongue from the reed. The tongue acts like a valve. Place the tongue on the reed, keeping the air pressure, then release. Continue in this fashion, as in figure 6.2.

Figure 6.2. Tongue While Keeping Air Pressure against Reed

3. In this exercise, try to keep the tongue relaxed so that is does not become muscle bound or tight. Use the weight of the tongue to tongue a series of notes. This is similar to the rebound stroke used on a snare drum, the stick being the tongue and the drumhead being the reed. In a rebound stroke, the weight of the stick after the first strike causes the next strike on the drumhead. This type of tongue stroke will help keep the tongue from becoming fatigued as fast. Try this using the examples in figure 6.3.

ARTICULATION

Figure 6.3. Rebound Tongue Stoke

4. Play the exercise in figure 6.4 using a single breath with a metronome setting of a quarter note equaling 60. When this can be played comfortably, move the metronome setting up a few beats. This may occur quickly at first, but do not be in a hurry to move the tempo up; you may spend several days at one tempo.

It is better to develop a good technique gradually than to hurry through and end up with uneven tonguing. If the passage becomes too difficult, back the metronome setting down by a few beats. When it then becomes easier, very gradually move the metronome setting up. By working on this tonguing technique consistently, one can improve the speed of one's tonguing. Note that as the speed of the tongue increases, the notes will have to become more staccato in nature. Always listen to the pitch! Fast tonguing is of no benefit if the fast notes are out of tune.

Figure 6.4. Increasing Tongue Speed

Tongue position is also important, not only for resonance when tonguing, but to help notes speak on time. In the diagram in figure 6.5, note the tongue position under each note, and the tongue position it refers to in figure 6.6. Position 1 uses an *Ah* position or open throat position. Position 4 is an *EEE* position in the throat, with the back of the tongue touching the molar teeth. Position 2 is used from low G (written) through the staff. Note that *v* in the diagram stands for the vent key or Ab/Eb key. This key helps with intonation and note stability in the altissimo register.

Figure 6.5. Note Range

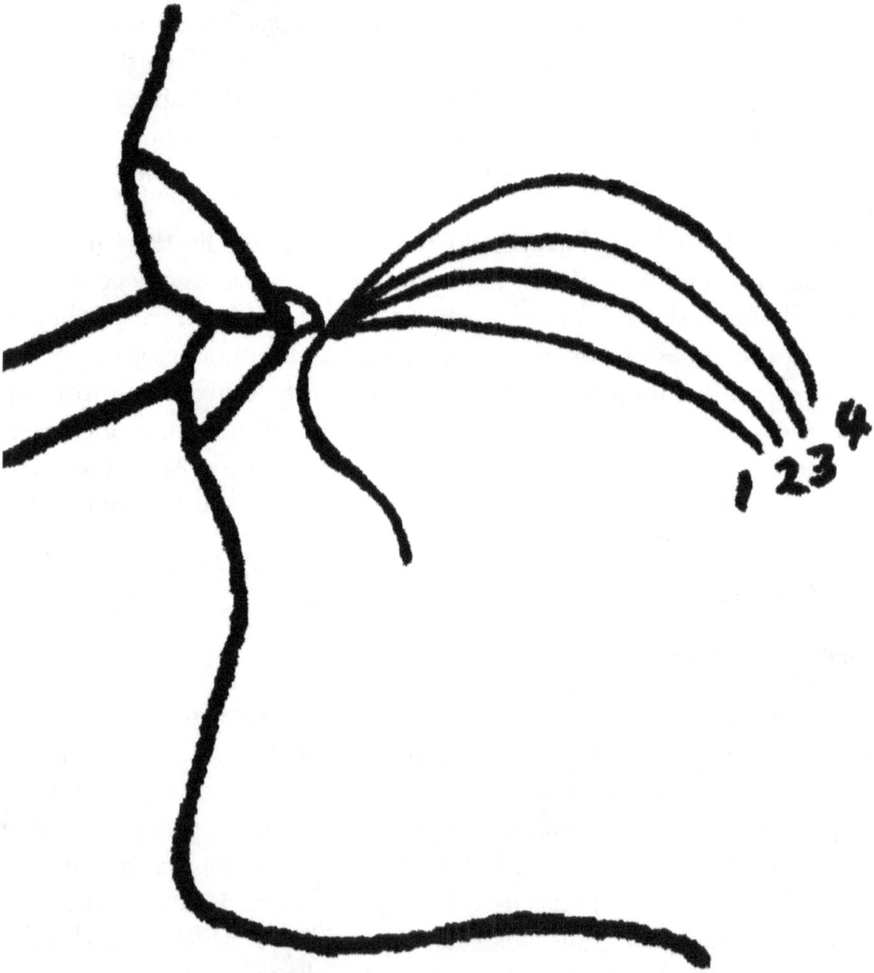

Figure 6.6. Tongue Position

7

FINGER TECHNIQUE

Finger technique must be developed to the point where the student is concentrating on making music and not worrying about playing notes. This is the goal of every musician and is the reason we practice, or should practice, often. The use of scales and etudes helps develop this technique. There are, however, some methods for achieving this end the student should observe. Mindful, deliberate practice is far more effective than careless repetition.

In playing technical passages involving many notes, make a conscious effort to *feel* every note, but avoid slamming the fingers onto the keys. All notes are important, though they may not be of equal stress or volume (as in the case of an accent or crescendo, for example).

Often, a scalar passage is easy, but wider intervals cause trouble, even though the fingering is no more difficult than the basic scale. Air technique or blowing technique is just as important as finger technique. When playing large interval leaps the tendency is to back off with the air pressure, thus the second note is often late in speaking. Take care to blow through the interval leap, especially a large leap. It may be necessary to crescendo during the interval to maintain the same volume between notes. If a diminuendo is marked at the point of a large interval leap up, one may wish to begin the diminuendo after the leap so that the top note of the leap does not drop out.

> **ADVANCED**
>
> When playing an interval that involves lifting many fingers, such as a third space C to the octave C above the staff, push very slightly with the right-hand thumb against the thumb rest, up toward the embouchure to set the mouthpiece slightly in the embouchure to produce a smooth interval change. This keeps the second note from popping out.

Every note must be heard in technical passages. One method to learn a difficult passage is to start with two notes in the middle of the line and add one note at a time on either side, developing a phrase from the center out. Only add notes after the first ones are mastered.

To even up a sixteenth note passage, practice by changing the rhythms from even sixteenth notes to dotted sixteenth, thirty-second (long-short) and then thirty-second, dotted sixteenth note (short-long). Then return to even sixteenth notes. See figure 7.1.

Try memorizing technical passages to get the eyes out of the music and the mind more into the music. (The other advantage of memorization is that when you memorize a passage, you truly know every note.) When learning a difficult four to eight note passage, memorize the motive, then shut your eyes and concentrate on feeling the fingers.

Take care not to breath pulse tied notes; that is, the listener should not hear a tie by virtue of the performer emphasizing that tied note with the breath. To avoid a breath pulse on a tied note, squeeze a finger

Practice this passage as follows, then return to original pattern.

Long-Short   Short-Long

Figure 7.1. Long-Short and Short-Long Pattern

FINGER TECHNIQUE

against the tone hole or key. Do not squeeze so much as to distort the tone, just a slight squeeze to *feel* the tied over note. Do not breath pulse dotted quarter notes.

Another practice technique is to group notes starting on the second or third note with the notes grouped into different sets of four notes. This changes the emphasis of the notes and helps prevent microscopic variations in time. The following passage, figure 7.2, from an unpublished Yost Clarinet Concerto, shows this regrouping. Notice that the re-beam example A starts on the fifth note of the original example. Example B starts on the fourth note of the original, and example C starts on the sixth note of the original.

All these practice techniques involve some form of variation or alteration of the original music. This compels the student to pay attention to every note all the time, and prevents careless errors from creeping into the performance unnoticed.

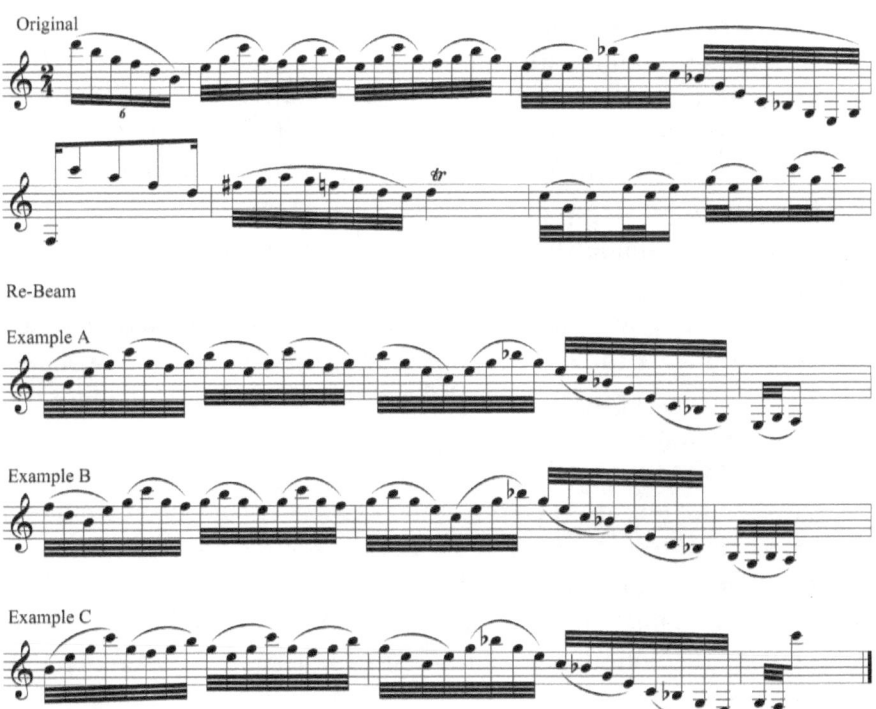

Figure 7.2.   Excerpt from Yost Concerto No. 8, Unpublished, from Author's Collection

With regard to the mechanics of finger technique, be sure when contacting the tone hole that the finger pad contacts the tone hole or rings around the tone hole evenly. The fingers should squarely contact the hole so that every edge of the tone hole is covered at the same time. The meaty part of the finger pad should sit in the tone hole for the most part. If one plays too much on the tips of the fingers, there may be difficulty covering the tone holes, and occasional leaks will cause squeaks, pitch variation, tonal variation, poor response, and even wrong notes. If played too far back, which is too close to the first knuckle, the fingers may also not seal to the tone hole and thus cause a leak.

The fingers should have a natural arch, the arch the fingers have when the hands are dropped relaxed to one's side. This arch is maintained for the clarinet hand position, as this is the shape that gives one the most strength. If you are trying to unscrew a cap from a jar, your fingers are not straight, but are curved. The fingers should pivot from the large knuckles, keeping this arched shape. The fingers must also track in a straight line up and down, staying above the tone hole or key. Any deviation from this path will slow the fingers down.

The same finger speed is used when the fingers go up as when the fingers go down. Attention should be paid to the upward finger movement, as this is usually the weakest in young students. Make sure the fingers do not fly up and straighten; just as with the tongue, the minimal motion should be used, as a large motion limits the potential rapidity of the technique. If there is a problem keeping the hand position or with fingers straightening out flat, try using masking tape around the fingers to tape the fingers into their proper curve shape. This is for practice purposes, in the practice room, to help obtain finger shape memory.

Take care not to slam the fingers onto the clarinet. This is more apparent when fingers are contacting the tone hole than when coming off the tone hole. Most students finger too heavily, slapping the keys and also creating tension in their wrists and hands. Think of a stream of water. You want to just touch the surface of the stream, and not go all the way down to the bottom or bed of the stream. In other words, finger on top the air-column.

The finger speed used in slow passages is the same finger speed as used in fast passages. If the fingers move 100 miles an hour between

FINGER TECHNIQUE

notes in a fast passage, they also move 100 miles an hour in a slow passage. The difference between the fast passage and the slow passage is the tempo of the pulse, not how notes change.

For legato slurred passages, try squeezing the fingers right before they come off the keys for intervals involving lifting two or more fingers. This can be particularly effective with an interval that requires lifting of fingers in both hands at the same time. This helps focus attention on the fingers that will come off the keys. This is most effective on fingers that cover tone holes, and less so for fingers that are pushing down keys (lever type keys). Think spongy fingers for legato passages, and for marcato passages think mechanical fingers (but not *slapping* fingers).

The hands or fingers should also be at a very slight angle to the keys so that there is minimal wrist movement to play the side keys. The wrists should be relatively straight to prevent problems from developing in the wrists. Students seem to have more wrist problems lately, but this may be more likely due to texting and computer usage, and not poor practice habits.

The right thumb should contact the thumb rest on the clarinet at the back of the right thumbnail or slightly behind, depending upon thumb length. Do not let the thumb rest sit on the thumb knuckle, as this will cause the hand position to lose the arch shape, making for pointy knuckles in the fingers.

The fingers should also stay within about a quarter of an inch of the tone holes or keys. If the fingers are raised too high, there is lost time involved in finger movement; and lost time equals slower fingers. Left thumb movement should be the same as for finger movement; do not slide or rock the left hand thumb off the thumbhole. Practice the following, beginning on first space F to open G: F–G, E–G, D–G, C–G. Pay particular attention to thumb movement.

Another fingering problem encountered with young students is that many will reach too high for the throat A-key. The index finger should only cover about the lower third of the key and should contact the key with the side of the finger. The key is a lever and will function no matter which part of it is pressed; it is unnecessary to reach all the way up to the middle of the key. A student who has worked hard to learn to cover open holes may develop the feeling that lever keys need to be pressed at their widest point.

> **BEGINNER**
>
> For proper finger position on the A-key, play F-sharp on the top (not side F-sharp) and rock the finger to the A-key. Be sure to come all the way off the first finger (F-sharp) hole. The index finger must be able to reach the first tone hole quickly and smoothly when coming off the A-key so as not to produce a gap or moment of silence when fingering notes following throat A.

The position of the right hand is most important, in part because it carries the weight of the clarinet; and because it carries the weight of the clarinet it is prone to having more problems than the left hand. Watch that the student does not rest the clarinet by sitting the side E-flat/B-flat key on the right-hand index finger. Some students will try to rest the right hand on the long rod of the bottom section and try to finger by moving at the middle finger joint rather than at the large knuckle. The right thumb supports the weight of the clarinet. All other digits must move freely.

It is perfectly acceptable for a student to hold the bell of the clarinet with the knees or to rest the bell on top of the knee when sitting. I still do after over forty years of playing, in part because of a double-jointed thumb that tires quickly when holding the weight of the clarinet. Just be careful not to cover the opening in the bell when playing F/C or B/E.

A student may also wish to use a neck strap when standing to play to take pressure off the thumb. I find that I lose about twenty percent of my technique due to tightness in my right forearm when standing and playing without a neck strap. The clarinet is a heavy instrument, and young players in particular can be discouraged from practicing by pain in their right thumbs. It is perfectly acceptable to also use a neck strap while seated.

A few specific suggestions here with regard to fingerings. When playing from third space C to Bb above the staff at a soft level, simply lift the middle finger of the left hand to finger the Bb. The Bb is therefore fingered: left hand, thumb-register-1-3, right hand 1-2-3-C key in the pinky. For a fast trill from G to A above the staff, finger G and simply trill the side Bb/Eb key in the right hand for the A.

FINGER TECHNIQUE

If playing a written high E above the staff (three leger line E) for a long period of time, finger it as: left hand, thumb-register key, 1-2-3 and the throat G# key. This works especially well if going from G (clarinet's third G) to E because you simply add the throat G# key to go from G to E a sixth higher. Be sure not to use the Ab/Eb vent key on C-sharp above the staff. Using the vent key here will cause C-sharp to be sharp on most clarinets. The vent key is used from D on up.

If trilling up a half step from C# to D, do not use the vent key on D. This is an awkward fingering and will slow down the trill. Also, in a situation where a student is playing a right-hand C in the staff to D above the staff, do not use the vent key. In other words, do not slide from the pinky C key to the pinky Ab/Eb vent key. The vent key is used to help high notes speak and to help some with intonation, depending upon the note.

Students should learn to use alternate fingerings in both the left and right pinky fingers at an early age. For example, B-D-F (starting on third-line B) is more evenly fingered if B is fingered in the right hand rather than the left hand. The more fingering one can keep in the same hand, the more even a passage will be.

The chromatic scale or chromatic passages should use trill fingerings, for the most part. Therefore, Eb/Bb in a chromatic passage is more even if played on top with the sliver key in the left hand than on the side with the right hand, since all the notes around it are in the left hand. Also, be sure to use forked B/F# in the right hand in a chromatic passage coming from Bb/F, as this is the trill fingering. Use the side F# and not the front F# (first space treble clef) in a chromatic passage as this is also the trill fingering.

Students learn better if they use all their senses, in other words, see it, hear it, do it. With this concept in mind, in order to get students to play smoother musical lines, have the student make a round, smooth circular

> **TEACHING TIP**
>
> It is much easier for a student to incorporate alternate fingerings from the beginning, when everything is new, than to learn with one set of fingerings and try to learn the alternates later.

motion with their arm. Now have the student play a scale with the same smooth motion in their playing. It may help for the teacher to make this circular motion while the student is playing the scale. This method can also be applied to technical passages that sound choppy or to melodic lines that need a smoother, flowing arch shape to the melodic phrase.

I studied with Clark Brody just after he retired from many years as principal clarinetist with the Chicago Symphony Orchestra. One of the first finger techniques he had me work on was what he called *Moving Fingers Ahead*. I remember M. F. A. written at the top of the page of the technical etudes from the Rose 32 and Rose 40 Etudes. Mr. Brody had learned this method of fingering from his clarinet teacher, Daniel Bonade.

This style of fingering is used for staccato passages. The idea is that when you staccato tongue a note, by the fact that it is staccato, there is a period of silence after the note. For example, a staccato quarter note sounds like an eighth note with an eighth rest after it, a staccato eighth note sounds like a sixteenth note with a sixteenth rest, etc.

The technique is that after you play a staccato note, you immediately finger the next note during the silence or rest that naturally occurs. Do not play the note until it is time for you to do so, though. If observing in slow motion, you will notice most students will keep the staccato note fingered until it is actually time to play the next note, then they finger that note.

The idea is that if you *pre-finger* the next note during the time that you are waiting for that next note to rhythmically occur, you will be able to increase your finger speed by simply removing the amount of silence between notes. You must practice this fingering technique by beginning at a very, very, slow tempo, like an eighth note at 50. It goes like this: Play the staccato note and stop sound with your tongue. Now finger (but do not play) the next note. Wait. Wait. Play this next staccato note and stop sound with your tongue. Now finger (but do not play) the next note. Wait. Wait. Now play this staccato note, etc.

One technique my father taught me to speed up my tongue was to double strike an eighth note passage. That is, for example, if playing eighth notes C-D-E, you play sixteenth notes C-C-D-D-E-E. Combining this technique and the Moving the Fingers Ahead technique, one would practice thirds in sixteenth notes, as shown in the following fig-

FINGER TECHNIQUE

ures. The original passage is in figure 7.3. Double strike this passage as in figure 7.4. Now practice moving to the next note during the rest, as indicated in figure 7.5. Remember to practice very slowly at first, then gradually speed up to the desired tempo.

You must remember when practicing that your mind and your brain are two separate entities. Your brain is going to work on instinct or reflexes whereas your mind is going to analyze that music and act accordingly. This is why it is important to practice slowly at first. When you practice slowly, this allows time for your mind to analyze the melodic structure, chord structure, fingerings, articulations, phrasing, etc. When you gradually speed up a passage, you are transferring data from what the mind has been developing into reflexes for the brain.

A seasoned professional musician may be able to do both at the same time, but for the average student, it is important not to skip slow practice of technical passages. Slow practice of technical passages is

Figure 7.3. Original Passage

Figure 7.4. Double Strike

Figure 7.5. Moving Fingers Ahead

the process of programming your brain with material the mind has developed.

Many things go into a good practice session. Is the correct note being played? Is this note at the correct pitch, with regard to intonation? The suggestion here is that the student practice with a tuner on the music stand and check notes from time to time. Are the rhythms correct? It may be helpful to record practice sessions and play the recording back, listening for rhythmical errors. Are dynamics at the correct level? Again, listening to a recording of oneself can help with this.

Does the musical phrase make sense? Does the musical line go toward a climactic point? Are the articulations correct? Do articulations vary so as to fit with the intent of the music? Is the music in the correct style? The student may need the help of a teacher who knows styles and literature for their particular instrument. Are correct fingerings being used in the correct spots? Again, the help of a teacher is a must.

Figures 7.6 and 7.7 show some of my favorite *trick* fingerings. The line between the numbers represents the division between the top and bottom sections of the clarinet.

TEACHING TIP

Students should be encouraged to study privately with a specialist on their instrument, as they will improve quicker than those who do not. As these students improve, so will the section in which they play. Students who are looking for private teachers may look to local colleges and universities, orchestras, and surrounding communities.

T=Left hand thumb   R=Register key   RH=Right Hand

LH=Left Hand   V = vent Ab/Eb key (RH pinky)

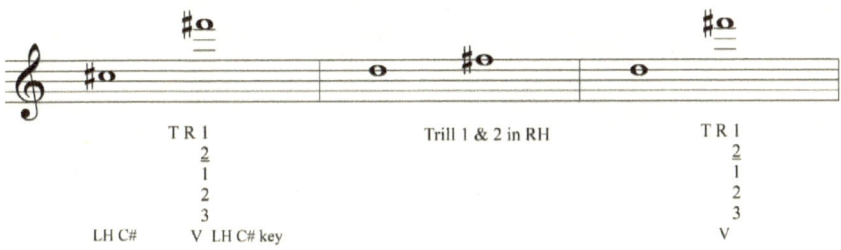

Figure 7.6. Fingerings 1.

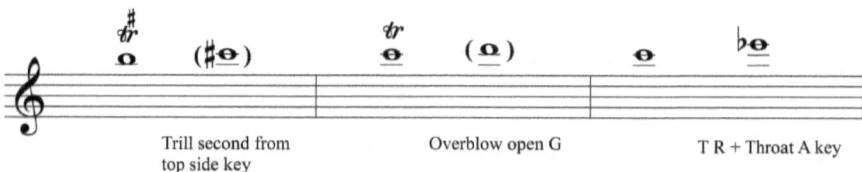
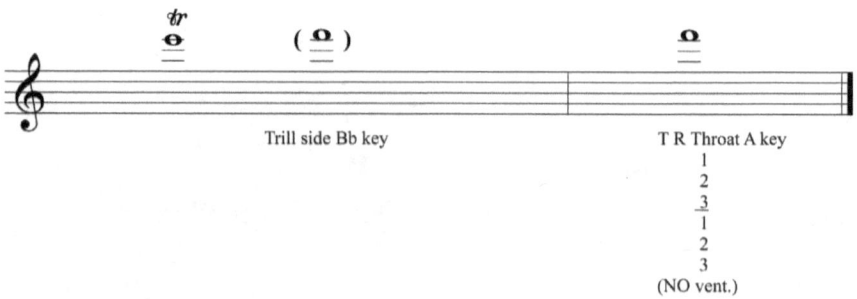

Figure 7.7. Fingerings 2.

8

MUSICALITY

Many musicians learn how to listen in an ensemble or solo rehearsal or performance, but have not learned how to listen in the practice room. Too often one *sees* on the page what one plays rather than *hears* what one plays. The musician in the practice room must learn to listen *between* notes. How does one note relate to the next? A series of notes in a musical phrase is like a series of words in a sentence. If one word does not make sense, or if the wrong word is emphasized, then the entire sentence may not make sense. If a note does not speak on time, is articulated poorly, is rhythmically incorrect, out of tune, at the wrong dynamic level, or of poor tone quality, the phrase is thus weakened.

Not all phrases will be played the same way. A phrase must have shape. It may have its high point or moment of intensity in the middle of the phrase, toward the beginning or end, or may be a series of high points. Of course, it is much easier to shape a phrase if one's technique is advanced enough not to get in the way of making music. However, students should develop their musicality hand-in-hand with their technique, and not delay phrasing as if it were some more advanced and difficult process for which they are not yet ready. Even a three-note melody such as *Mary Had a Little Lamb* can be played with musical expression.

> **BEGINNER**
>
> Play the first measure of a piece of music in your mind before you start to play it on your instrument. You can also put the instrument down and sing the melody, listening for your instinctive phrasing. It is practically impossible to sing without creating some sort of natural phrase.

The musician must think of music as an art form. Think of a piece of music like a beautiful marble sculpture. One does not see chips in a fine work of art, and one should not hear *chips*, that is, poor interval changes, poor articulation, and so on, within a piece of music. Many musicians could use more refinement, finesse, and general smoothness in their playing. When in doubt, be musical. Do not let technical passages substitute for musicality. Even though a passage may be technical, it must still sound musical.

It helps if the student is encouraged to play technical exercises, such as scales, arpeggios, and intervals, as musically as if they were composed melodies. One method to practice a technical passage or movement, such as the third movement of a concerto, is to slow the passage down to half tempo. Practice the passage at this slow tempo making it as musical as possible, to the point of overdoing the musicality. Then take the passage or movement back up to tempo, but still attempt to keep the musicality. In this way, a section that may have originally sounded like a finger exercise will sound musical even if it is a technical finger passage.

Playing a piece of music can be divided into three stages. Stage number one is playing what one *thinks* is on the page. Generally, the student will underplay dynamics. A dynamic change that *feels* extreme to the student might be barely noticeable from across the room. He or she may also not play accurate articulations or may play inaccurate rhythms. Have the student record herself and play the recording back while watching the music. The student then should write down on a piece of paper what she can do to improve her performance. Take the paper to the practice room and make adjustments.

Stage number two is playing what *is* on the page. This is what most musicians want to do and most are satisfied to play what is on the page. However, this is just the start to playing musically. The composer cannot put every musical nuance onto the page. There simply is not enough

MUSICALITY

room or musical symbols available. Some musical aspects must be left to the performer. This is what makes one performer's rendition of a particular piece different from another's of the same piece.

Also, in the Baroque and early Classical stylistic periods, composers typically left most dynamics, ornaments, and even articulations to the performer's discretion. A musician who plays only what is on the page is not fulfilling the composer's intentions.

Stage number three is playing *beyond* what is on the page. All musicians should strive for this stage. Playing musically requires playing beyond what is on the page. The performer must put warmth and life into symbols found on a piece of paper. This is the essence of making music.

All too often, students are too tied to the music that is on the page. They are afraid to let the music come to life. They think if they do something that is not in the music, a slight pulling back of the tempo or pushing forward, for example, that this is not allowed. Do not let what is on the page get in the way of making music. The following suggestions can help one to play beyond what is on the page.

Play *kinetic* phrases, especially in solo playing. That is, play with movement toward a goal, toward a climactic point or high point of the phrase, or toward a conclusion. Do not sit on long notes within a phrase; do something with the note—a crescendo, a diminuendo, a combination of crescendo and diminuendo, use vibrato, do something so as not to let the energy of the phrase die. It is okay, however, to sit on a long note at the high point of the phrase, to show that you have reached the *top of the mountain*.

If you do not know what to do with a musical line, try a crescendo as the line goes up the scale and a diminuendo as the line goes down the scale. If you are trying to make a musical phrase more intense, make up a story to go with it that matches what you are trying to do (happy, sad, angry, dramatic, etc.). Try to play the line to reflect the story.

Another method is to find the primary notes of a melody. Relate this to a sentence. For example, equate the following sentence to primary notes: *There is a frog in the road. Frog* and *road* are probably the most important words in the sentence and your voice should emphasize these two words. Now ornament the sentence with additional words to produce: *There is a big green fat frog in the wide slippery road.* Notice how this works with the following four-measure motive. In the motive in

Figure 8.1. Four Measure Motive

figure 8.1, the student will crescendo to or slightly accent or emphasize the third note in each measure.

Now this motive is ornamented with additional notes to produce a familiar tune by Beethoven. Still, crescendo to or aim for the third beat in each measure in the following example shown in figure 8.2.

An additional thing to consider is to always overdo the dynamics. What you may hear with the horn in your hands may not be what the audience hears several yards from you. Remember what your teachers told you at a young age: play to the back of the room so that the people farthest away do not have to strain to hear you. With this in mind, one may also have to overdo the musical aspects of a piece, not only the dynamics.

Even accompaniment lines should be played musically, although the accompaniment should always be subordinate to the solo; even whole notes can be well phrased, with clean, controlled beginnings and endings, and thorough control of the dynamics.

Use the same breath support for soft passages as for loud passages. Soft passages do not require you to blow as hard, but the sound still needs to be maintained with proper embouchure technique and air that is supported from the diaphragm, not shallow chest breathing. Your body is part of your instrument. Think of blowing from your abdominal muscles through the instrument, all the way to the bell and slightly beyond.

When playing a rising half-step at a cadence, give a little push to the second-to-last note. Avoid any key noise or sounds at the ends of phrases that may distract from the music. Do not accent or land

Figure 8.2. Ornamented Four-Measure Motive, Beethoven Symphony No. 9, Fourth Movement

> **ADVANCED**
>
> Sing the phrase, and then play the phrase. Many people will naturally sing with more emotion than when they play.

heavy on the last note of the phrase, that is, the cadence note. The only exception to this rule is if the composer has specifically marked an accent on the last note. In general, there is a slight diminuendo or *rounding off* of the last note of a phrase. It is like a period in a sentence. The listener should know you have finished the phrase, just as a speaker finishes a sentence.

If working on solo material, it is a good idea to play from the piano part a few times (if the clarinet part above the piano score is transposed to the clarinet key). Keep an eye on the piano accompaniment. This is one way to learn the accompaniment. A soloist should always know the accompaniment. Another method to learn the accompaniment and to get different interpretations of the solo is to listen to a variety of recordings while watching the piano score. A good method of practicing is to record yourself and play the recording back at half speed, listening for even runs and clean technique.

Students should be aware of some basic ornamentation symbols and how to perform them, as the following show in figure 8.3.

 Acciaccatura: a fast grace note.

 Appoggiatura: slightly accented grace note.

 Turn above note.

 Turn between notes.

 Turn with accidental above turn.

 Inverted turn. Sometimes also written as an upside down turn.

 Short hand notation.

 Mordent: Single trill up. Inverted Mordent: Single trill down.

Figure 8.3. Ornamentation Symbols

9

A COLORFUL WARM-UP ROUTINE

This warm-up routine is a fun way to vary the warm-up process each day. Warming up before practicing is the same as warming up before exercising. Warming up allows the embouchure and the fingers to *stretch*, as well as allowing the ears and mind to get into the correct state or *frame of mind* for the music to come.

In this warm-up routine, the student selects a color, maybe to match his or her mood, maybe the first color the student sees in the morning, or maybe just pull a random colored strip of paper or colored pencil from a box. The student then matches the selected color with the color from the following list. Each colored routine has an area of concentration: for example, tone, articulation, finger accuracy, chord structure, rhythm, or meter. Each color also emphasizes a particular scale and has a warm-up exercise focusing on the mentioned areas of concentration.

YELLOW

In this warm-up exercise, figure 9.1, concentrate on a good tone. Try to achieve a sound that has a dark center with resonance. Be sure to use a

CHAPTER 9

Figure 9.1. Yellow

good embouchure with a focused sound. If needed, review the chapter on embouchure. Use a full breath. Do not shallow breathe or chest breathe, but fill the entire set of lungs with air.

RED

In this warm-up exercise, listen to how chords are formed through the use of a three-note chord called a triad. By adding a fourth note to top of a triad, a chord called a seventh chord is produced. See if you can hear the difference between a triad and a seventh chord in figure 9.2.

A COLORFUL WARM-UP ROUTINE

Figure 9.2. Red

BLUE

In the warm-up exercise in figure 9.3, the student will explore the blues scale and play a twelve-bar blues tune. Pay particular attention to articulation. As with all the warm-up exercises, articulations may be varied for variety.

GREEN

The warm-up exercise in figure 9.4 stresses finger speed as well as trills. Listen for clean, precise finger action. Use techniques found in chapter 7 on finger technique.

Figure 9.3. Blue

ORANGE

Rhythm is one of the most important aspects of music. This warm-up exercise, figure 9.5, emphasizes dotted rhythms and triplets. Be sure *not* to play a dotted eighth-sixteenth note figure as a quarter-eighth note triplet figure. Try stressing or slightly accenting the weak part of the beat in syncopated passages to help bring out the feeling of syncopation.

BROWN

Meter is closely related to rhythm. In this warm-up exercise, figure 9.6, the student practices counting through a series of meter changes in both simple and compound meter.

Figure 9.4. Green

Figure 9.5. Orange

Figure 9.6. Brown

72 CHAPTER 9

> **TEACHING TIP**
>
> The band director may transpose any of these warm-up exercises into different keys for added variety. Begin with the easier keys, and then move out into more difficult keys as the students progress. If the clarinet section is out of tune, try playing the chorale in figure 9.7 and having the students listen for intonation.

WARM-UP INTONATION EXERCISE

To work on intonation, try placing a tuner on the stand with a drone tone sounding, for example, a concert B-flat. Start on the dominant (the fifth degree above the tuning note or fourth degree below) and play up

Figure 9.7. Warm-Up Chorale

A COLORFUL WARM-UP ROUTINE

to the drone tone. If the drone tone or tuning note is concert B-flat, start at concert F and play up to the Bb (F-G-A-Bb). Listen to the intonation for the third below the Bb (the G) as you play up to the Bb. Start once again on the dominant, but this time play down to the tuning note or drone tone (F-E-D-C-Bb). This time listen to the third above the tuning note (the D in our example), as well as the tuning note itself.

While warming up as a section, one person can play the drone tone while another plays up and down to it. You can download a cello drone tone if you prefer something a little warmer than the tuner's note. If you have access to a piano that is in tune, pick out a tuning note or drone tone on the piano, play that note and hold down the sustain pedal. Start on the dominant and play up and down to the sustained note. You can also play a triad based off the sustained note. In the above example, the notes will be Bb-D-F (C-E-G when transposed to B-flat clarinet).

Be aware of the fact that when you hold down the sustain pedal on the piano, some strings will vibrate in sympathy with the vibrations produced by your clarinet. This will not be the case if you use an electric piano or synthesizer. If using a synthesizer or a note produced by a computer, you may want to try using a cello tone as it may prove to be a little warmer sounding and less synthetic.

10

REHEARSING THE WOODWIND SECTION

INTONATION

The students will find it helpful to have a group warm-up before playing their music in rehearsal, just as choirs do. This allows them a few minutes to warm up physically and to make sure their instruments are working. It also gives them time to adjust their minds from whatever activity preceded band and lets them start thinking musically without the stress of "performing" for the band director. Additionally, a group warm-up at the downbeat of class time gets the students playing right away, and keeps them from wasting rehearsal time in chatting and socializing.

Check intonation within each woodwind section, and then check intonation between sections. This may be done with individual notes or with a chord. For example, the saxophones could play the root, the clarinets, the third, and the double reeds and flutes, the fifth. Mix this up with other various combinations. *Always have the students sit up straight using good posture, as poor posture produces poor intonation.*

Woodwinds will go sharp in warm weather and flat in cold weather. Strings and the piano do just the opposite, and this could become an issue when woodwinds and strings or piano are playing together. Students should tune at a mezzo-forte dynamic, as soft and loud dynamics can

> **BEGINNER**
>
> When the pitch is sharp, one must pull at the proper location (see individual instrument intonation), and when flat, one must push in.

cause pitch problems, as will be discussed later. If students are having intonation problems, have them sing their parts. Watch for the following pitch tendencies throughout the rehearsal.

Flute Intonation

The flute is made so that the head joint may be pulled one-eighth to three-sixteenths of an inch for intonation purposes. Flutes can go flat in the low register, and sharp in the high register. Soft passages can go flat while loud passages can go sharp. The student who is sharp should blow more down into the flute embouchure plate hole, while the student who is flat should try to blow more across the plate.

Make sure the end cork on the head joint is 17 millimeters from the center of the hole in the lip plate. The flute's cleaning rod should have a groove on it that can be used to measure this by placing the rod inside the head joint and sighting the groove in the middle of the lip plate hole. Double-check to make sure the groove on the rod is 17 millimeters from the end of the rod. If the end cork is set too close to the hole in the lip plate, it throws the high register and low register into opposite directions with regard to intonation.

Lack of breath support can also cause the pitch to go flat on the flute. Open C and C# have a tendency to go sharp. Blowing down into the flute too much can cause the pitch to go flat. Embouchure plays a big

> **TEACHING TIP**
>
> Sometimes young students will unscrew the end cork and change this set-up. If the end cork is loose, take it to a repair technician and ask that hot wax be used to place the cork in the proper position.

role with regard to flute intonation. More air speed is needed for high notes, which may be attained by making the embouchure hole slightly smaller while using the same volume of air.

Flute players must have a clean, clear tone in order to check intonation. Fuzzy flute tones are generally caused by the opening in the lips being too big, of the wrong size, or because the hole on the embouchure plate of the flute and the embouchure are not parallel to each other. The center of the embouchure should feel relaxed. This is done by applying pressure only in the corners of the lips and forcing air through the center of the lips to create the proper opening.

Oboe Intonation

The oboe's lowest notes can go flat while the middle register can be sharp. Oboists can roll (not slide) the reed in and out of the embouchure slightly to adjust pitch. If flat, roll the reed/horn into the mouth, thus making the horn shorter and the pitch higher. If sharp, roll the reed/horn out of the mouth, making the oboe longer and thus lower in pitch. The oboist should never adjust pitch by pulling the reed out of the instrument or pulling the sections of the instrument apart. An oboe reed should crow a C. Crowing is a raspy sound produced when blowing only the reed, thereby causing both blades of the reed to vibrate.

In case of poor intonation, check for a proper embouchure. The lower lip should try to *cup* as much of the lower lip as possible *around* the reed to get the lip on the sides of the reed and less simply up and downward pressure. Keep the angle of the oboe a little higher than a clarinet angle (slightly above 45 degrees) so that air flow is contacting both blades of

---

TEACHING TIP

The oboist should not adjust pitch by pulling the reed in and out of the instrument. The reed should always be pushed all the way into the oboe, so there is no gap between the receiver of the oboe and the staple/reed. Find a brand of reed that works for both tone and intonation, and stay with that brand. If there are pitch problems, slightly roll the reed on the embouchure in or out as discussed previously.

the reed and not mostly on the lower blade. Keep the tongue low in the mouth to blow warm air, as if saying *ah* in the throat, or think of keeping an *open* throat to help with pitch. Sometimes the only solution to poor intonation is a new reed. An oboe student should always have at least three playing reeds.

Clarinet Intonation

See chapter 5. The bass clarinet pulls at the neck if sharp, not the mouthpiece. Double-check this position as rehearsal continues. Sometimes the tightening screw that holds the neck in place will loosen and the neck will gradually slide down during the course of a rehearsal. To assure the proper amount of embouchure pressure is used, when playing the bass clarinet mouthpiece and reed alone, the pitch produced should be an F-sharp.

Clarinetists who double on saxophone may have a tendency to play sharp on the saxophone. This is because a tighter embouchure is used on clarinet than on saxophone, so the clarinetist will have a tendency to pinch more. The saxophone also blows about half the air pressure than that of the clarinet, so clarinetists are used to blowing harder.

Bassoon Intonation

The low notes on bassoon can be sharp while the upper register can go flat. Soft passages tend to be sharp and loud passages tend to go flat. The bassoon reed should *crow* below an F; and as on the oboe, the reed crows showing that both blades are vibrating when the reed is played alone. If the reed plays a clear single tone, then only one blade is vibrating and the embouchure may not be straddling the crow point. If this is the case, check that the student is using a proper embouchure.

The upper lip should be in front of the bottom lip, creating an overbite. The aim is to straddle the crow point of the reed. The upper lip should also be firmer than the bottom lip and should almost touch the first wire. Keep the lips round and full-bodied, or wrinkled. In other words, do not try to stretch the lips thin. A good embouchure helps with both intonation and tone. Of course, the student must be playing on a reed of proper length and proper hardness.

> **TEACHING TIP**
>
> If a reed is too soft and may be playing flat, squeeze the first wire (closest to tip) on the sides to open the distance between the blades, making the reed stiffer and raising the pitch. If the reed is too stiff, and possibly playing sharp, squeeze the first wire on the top and bottom to close the distance between the blades, thus making the reed easier to blow and lowering the pitch. It is suggested that small toothless needle-nose pliers be used.

Make sure the bassoonist adjusts his or her seat strap so that the bocal/reed swings directly into the mouth. The student should not raise or lower the head to reach the reed. As with the oboe, no part of the bassoon can be pulled out or in to adjust the pitch; however, most bassoons come with two bocals, one shorter and one longer. Because the bassoon is more likely to go sharp than flat, the student should routinely play on the shorter bocal, which is probably marked 2, and switch to the longer bocal, which is probably marked 3, on days when the room is hot or the reed is playing sharp.

Saxophone Intonation

Soft dynamics on the saxophone tend to go sharp while loud dynamics go flat. Low notes can be flat (although low B and B-flat may be sharp) and the high register tends to go sharp. Fourth line written D tends to be sharp. Tune to three finger G (both octaves), and if sharp, pull the mouthpiece out; if flat, push the mouthpiece in. Never pull at the neck to tune the saxophone.

For proper embouchure pressure and thus proper pitch, playing only the alto saxophone mouthpiece and reed should produce the pitch A. A tenor saxophone mouthpiece and reed produce a G, and the baritone saxophone mouthpiece and reed, a D. The saxophone embouchure should use a natural shape chin, do not try to flatten it out as one does on the clarinet. It is okay to use a little more bottom lip on the reed than one would use on the clarinet embouchure, but still do not allow the flesh-colored part of the lip to sit on the reed because the muscle is in the red portion of the lip.

Be sure saxophone players keep an open throat, keeping the tongue low in the mouth (as if saying *ah*), while in the low and middle ranges. This is like blowing warm air to warm up your hands. In the altissimo range, students may need to raise the tongue to more of an *EE* position, with the back of the tongue almost touching the back molar teeth. This helps to move the air faster for the altissimo register. If playing too soft a reed or playing with too loose an embouchure, the pitch tends to go flat. If the reed is too hard, causing the student to pinch or bite, the pitch will tend to go sharp.

Tune octaves, thirds, and fifths between sections. In spots where alternate fingerings are possible, make sure that students are using the same fingering within each section: for example, a middle finger F-sharp versus a forked F-sharp. Saxophonists should not slide to or off the *bis* key when going between B natural to B-flat; the student should use the one and one B-flat fingering or the side B-flat fingering. Only slide where there are rollers between keys.

TONE

Each instrument should be in tune when using its best tone. Good tone helps intonation. Darker tones in the reeds will blend better than bright tones. Be sure instruments within a section and between sections agree when and where to use vibrato. Saxophones should use a jaw vibrato while double reeds use a diaphragmatic vibrato. Flutists also use a vibrato that is produced from the diaphragm, but some feel it as being a little higher up in the chest than a double reed player's vibrato. Clarinets should not use vibrato unless specifically called for in the score.

Tone is a very important aspect of practicing and rehearsing, which is often forgotten about or given second place to working out notes and rhythm. The concept of tone may vary between countries or even regions within a country. In fact, different styles of playing, for example jazz versus *classical*, may involve different types of tone. However, one must play with a pleasing sound or nobody will want to listen.

With regard to a jazz tone and a classical or traditional tone, I recommend that clarinet and saxophone students use two different reed and mouthpiece set-ups. For a jazz or Dixieland clarinet tone, clarinetists

> **BEGINNER**
>
> While it is tempting to save good reeds for concerts and use poorer-sounding reeds for practicing, one cannot improve one's tone quality without practicing on a quality-sounding, responsive reed. This is not to say that you use your very best reeds for practicing. Do save a couple of your best reeds for concerts, but try not to use poor sounding and responding reeds at all. These reeds should be discarded so that one is not tempted to fall back on them.

may try using a lighter reed with a more open mouthpiece. A few words here with regard to a traditional clarinet tone. Although there are many different concepts of tone, generally a traditional clarinet sound strives for a dark centered tone. The clarinetist may want to try to imitate a good dark, warm cello tone.

For saxophone players, a jazz set-up uses a jazz mouthpiece and a reed with a little less heart that is a little brighter, able to hold its own with the brass section, and articulate easily allowing for glissandos and other jazz techniques. The more traditional saxophone tone uses a darker mouthpiece and reed combination. Using these two set-ups allows for two separate and distinct sounds.

RHYTHM

Work for accurate subdivisions of the beat. Pay particular attention to tied notes. Be sure that the dotted eighth-sixteenth note figure is not played as a triplet figure. Watch that the first note of a sixteenth note passage is not rushed and that the second and third notes are clean. When entering after a short rest where the rest occurs on the downbeat, do not breathe on the beat, as the entrance may be late and thus distort the rhythm. Just because there is a rest does not mean one needs to take a breath.

Play difficult rhythms on a unison pitch; master the rhythm first, and then add the pitches. If a rhythm is particularly challenging, put the instrument down and learn the rhythm while clapping, tapping, or vocalizing. Technically demanding passages should be rehearsed at

> **TEACHING TIP**
>
> Sometimes thinking of the syllables of a word can help keep rhythms even. For example, for triplet figures, try using the three syllable word *Florida*. For a set of sixteenth notes, one may use *Mississippi*, and for a quintuplet, the word *opportunity*. Sometimes low notes in the double reeds and saxophones may be late speaking and thus distort the rhythm. Students tend to back away from challenging passages and entrances; encourage them to play a little louder on these difficult entrances, as that will make the low notes easier.
>
> **BEGINNER**
>
> For clarinetists, sometimes notes may be late speaking when going over the break (going from third line B-flat to B-natural). To help with this, do not back off on breath support. Make sure all fingers contact the keys at the same time. Try not to consciously adjust the embouchure; any change in embouchure is very minute.

a very slow tempo. Do not breath pulse tied and dotted notes. When playing a dotted eighth-sixteenth note figure, hold the dotted eighth for its full value rather than playing an eighth note followed by a sixteenth rest followed by the sixteenth note. The exception to this is in staccato passages.

When playing a dotted eighth-sixteenth note figure in close proximity to eighth note triplets, play a double dotted eighth note–thirty second note figure to better distinguish it from a triplet figure. Sometimes dotted eighth-sixteenth note figures get lazy and sound like quarter note-eighth note triplet figures.

ARTICULATION

Check to see that note lengths are held for full value and that note lengths are agreed upon between sections, especially the length of staccato notes. Oboe and bassoon players can play a quicker staccato than can single reed players. Clarinetists can generally play quicker staccato notes than can saxophone players. Within the section, alto saxophone players can play quicker staccato notes than tenor or baritone saxophonists. Tenor and baritone saxophonists may have to play more on top of the beat than the alto section because the larger reed and horn can require more air and a quicker articulation. The smaller the instrument, generally the quicker the response time.

Check to see that legato articulations agree both within a section and between sections. Pay particular attention that phrase endings agree between woodwind sections and that any passages that are imitated between sections agree.

Make sure that articulations are stylistically accurate. For example, the downbeat of a waltz will be slightly accented on the first beat of the measure, which will be different from a march. Articulations in a march may be a little more marcato than that of a chamber piece, for example by Mozart. A staccato in a slow movement is a longer note than a staccato in a fast movement. Do not accent grace notes that come before the beat.

Avoid accenting downbeats, especially in the case of two sets of four-sixteenth notes. In this case, try to play two sets of four sixteenth notes as if it was one set of eight sixteenth notes. However, sometimes it is helpful to emphasize the bottom note of an arpeggio to *spring* through the run in fast passages. Slightly accenting or stressing syncopated upbeat figures can help to bring out the syncopation. When tonguing repeated notes, make sure all notes are heard equally, not just the first note. Think about the release of a note, not just the attack. Sometimes the release of one note is the attack of the next note.

ADVANCED

Clarinetists may find a more legato interval when jumping to a C-sharp or D above the staff by rolling the first finger in the left hand off the first tone hole, rather than simply lifting it off.

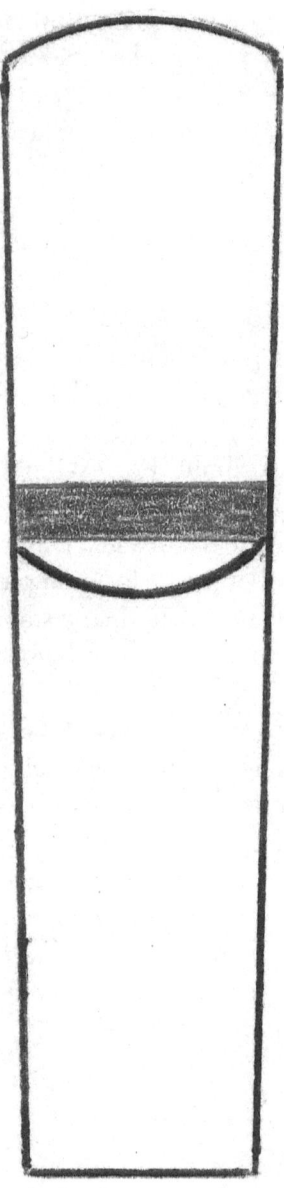

Figure 10.1. Low Note Scrape Area

Low notes on saxophone are difficult to play and thus may be late speaking. One reason is that the low note pads are on the largest part of the horn and may require a little more air. The other is that the large pad cups easily get bumped and can leak. A repair technician can drop a leak-light down the horn and look for light leaking from around a pad. If the horn is not leaking, then sometimes *a little* wood may need to be removed from the reed just in front of where the cut begins, as in the shaded area of figure 10.1. This will help balance the reed. However, if the reed is too soft, high notes will be difficult to play.

Make sure that the weight of the saxophone is on the neck strap. If the student tries to carry the weight of the horn on the thumb, this can affect how a note speaks. If the saxophone is played to the side (the alto may be played in front or on the side whereas tenor and baritone are played on the side), be sure the mouthpiece enters the student's embouchure evenly. That is, the student should not tilt his or her head to the left, but rather turn the mouthpiece to the right so that the mouthpiece enters the embouchure evenly. When standing, the length of the neck strap may need to be adjusted differently from where it is when sitting.

If a saxophone neck is missing part of its cork at the end, the part that lies under the mouthpiece, this may cause the reed to squeak and notes to speak late. This is due to a gap between the cork and the inside of the mouthpiece. Have the cork replaced as soon as possible. For a temporary fix, wrap the missing cork area with electrical tape.

> **TEACHING TIP**
>
> Do not drop the jaw to get low notes to speak. Instead, try a slight pressure with the right thumb pushing against the body of the saxophone when descending to low B and Bb.

DYNAMICS

Be sure all woodwind players agree as to how loud or soft a *forte* or *piano* is going to be within the context of a particular piece. Remind students that each dynamic has a range within that dynamic and that it is not one specific volume. Be sure all members of the ensemble know who has the melody and secondary melody and when and where it occurs. Pay particular attention to the dynamic level of any motive or melody that is passed from one section to another. Do not let it drop out or lose intensity as it is passed between sections. As they learn a piece of music, students should always be aware of the melody, especially if they are not playing it themselves.

Loud volumes in the low register are difficult on flute. Soft volumes in the low register are difficult on saxophone and oboe. Loud volumes are limited in the throat tones (G#, A, Bb) in the clarinets. Soft articulations are difficult on the oboe and bassoon, and easy for the flute and clarinet. Because each section has its own challenges and limitations, the dynamic effect of the ensemble will be a compromise between what is ideal and what is possible.

> **TEACHING TIP**
>
> Sometimes the sax G# pad sticks and does not open when G-sharp is fingered. If this happens, pull a dollar bill under the sticky G# pad. With regard to saxophone or a bass clarinet where the neck goes into the body, do not use cork grease where metal touches metal; instead use oil. Cork grease can collect dust or dirt fragments that may scratch the metal. The same is true for flute joints. Cork grease is only for corks.

> **BEGINNER**
>
> Do not play loud dynamics to the point where the tone becomes bad. Also, do not loosen the embouchure and drop the pitch to get louder—simply blow harder.

ENSEMBLE

Entrances must be clear. Make sure long held notes get out of the way of moving lines. Phrases should aim for a climactic point and the interpretation of the phrase should be consistent between sections. There is a big difference between *what's that in the road ahead?* and *what's that in the road, a head?*

Take breaths in logical places. Do not breathe a few notes before a cadence. That would be like breathing before the last word in a sentence if you were talking. Do not break a sequential pattern by breathing. It is almost always wrong to breathe on a bar line, unless the phrase clearly ends at that point. Generally, steal time from the note before the breath so that the downbeat after the breath is on time. If entering on a high note pay particular attention to the pitch. Hear the pitch in your head before you enter.

Do not breathe through the nose, but breathe through the mouth with an open throat, as if yawning. Students must learn to take in as much air as quickly as they can. The shoulders should not rise when a student takes in a breath. Fill up the entire lungs; feel like you are filling the lungs from the bottom up. The diaphragm should expand; in other words, do not shallow or chest breathe.

Sometimes there is not enough time to take a full breath. It is okay to take a half breath or a series of half breaths if the phrasing allows. Sometimes oboists will take a little longer to breathe because they do not use up all their air and must exhale old air before taking in new. Flutists, on the other hand, use up their air quickly and need to breathe more often than reed players. The instrument needs a constant and consistent air supply that is controlled; it is the students' responsibility to give this to the instrument. Think of the airflow as pushing forward like water flowing without any ripples.

When a breath mark is indicated in the music, it is not necessarily there for the convenience of the performer; sometimes it marks a point where the composer wants a very slight pause in the phrase. This equates to a comma in a text. The phrase does not taper off in volume like it does at the end of the phrase, but rather time is generally taken from the preceding note as one would if breathing at that point. Even if the performer does not need to breathe, the same amount of time required to take a breath should be taken at that point, as the breath mark is used as a phrasing mark. This phrasing mark, or comma in a musical phrase, is called an *einschnitt*.

There should be a blend and balance not only within sections, but also between sections. Watch that the low saxophones do not play behind the beat. Saxophone players often have trouble with left-hand palm keys, that is, the notes D to F above the staff. They should therefore spend more time working on these notes and seek out exercises that develop palm key technique so ensemble playing stays clean.

Think of a phrase as continuing into the rest. That is not to say playing during the rest, but the silence of the rest is part of the phrase. This will help students not to chop phrase endings or lose control of the pitch at the end of the note. Make sure students are using alternate or chromatic fingerings in the correct situations. Check to see that music stands are not too low. If the stand is too low and the student is looking down, the embouchure may be distorted, tonguing may be difficult, and the student will have to look too far up from the music to see the director.

Sometimes fingers and tongue do not coordinate, that is, they simply get apart. Although many students blame their tongue, it is often the fact that the fingers are not even. The fingers are leaping all over the place playing notes, but the tongue is able to sit in one location keeping even articulations. The best way to line up the tongue and the fingers is to practice the passage slurred. Once the passage can be performed evenly slurred, add the tongue back in. Usually the tongue and fingers will then line up.

A slur over staccato notes will be played as legato-tongued notes for the most part in solo playing, but in an ensemble, the legato tongue

> **BEGINNER**
>
> When sitting for long rests, remove the mouthpiece from your mouth to allow the blood flow to return to the lips. When entering after a long rest, bring the instrument back to playing position several seconds before your entrance.

may be lost. It is best to play these as normal tongued notes when in an ensemble.

Music consists largely of patterns. Point out patterns in the music, particularly between sections, and patterns or motives that might be passed back and forth between sections. Memorizing a piece of music may be easier if one can see how patterns connect together.

SECTION LEADER

The role of the section leader is very important. Not every detail can be covered by the director during a rehearsal. Section players should look to the section leader for balance, dynamics, articulation, consistency with the section, etc. When in doubt, follow the lead of the section leader. Sometimes it may be necessary to make slight adjustments, for example, in the length of staccato articulations when playing in an unfamiliar concert hall that is very resonant. It is the section leader who may have to provide guidance for such quick adjustments at a rehearsal.

As section leader, do not be afraid to give slight cues if needed within the section; nothing big that distracts from a performance or draws attention to you, just subtle cues to help the section stay together. It is also the section leader's job to see that everyone is sitting on the front edge of their seats, not all the way back against the back rest.

11

PREPARING FOR A SOLO PERFORMANCE

When preparing for a solo performance, a number of factors in addition to the preparation of the music must be taken into consideration. Of first concern is the physical stamina required to perform, especially if the performance is a concerto with the band or an entire solo concert. Long brisk walks or some type of aerobics is particularly helpful, especially if physical education classes have been reduced in your school district.

Staying in physical shape includes keeping your embouchure in shape. This is done by practicing in forty-five-minute intervals with sufficient rest between practice sessions. Do not adjust your practice routine as the performance approaches. Increasing practice time a few days before a performance may make for a weak lip on performance day. The same thing may happen if you reduce practice time a few days before the performance. However, on the day of the performance, it is suggested that you keep practice to a minimum. If you do not know the piece by the day of the performance, it is too late to learn it.

You should, however, spend about five minutes warming up before the performance, if for no other reason than intonation. Last-minute technical practice does more harm than good, especially if you run through the fast passages at top speed. If there is a particularly frightening passage, play it with a beautiful tone at half speed three times and then leave it alone. The worst thing one can do is to play through a tough passage ten minutes before a performance and mess it up. All you will think about during the performance is that passage and whether you will mess it up when it rears its ugly head.

Be sure to practice under the same conditions as you will perform. For example, if you are going to play standing up, you must practice standing up. Standing slightly changes the balance of the body, and difficult technical passages will feel different. Standing also uses more energy, and you may find you need to plan different breaths during long passages to account for the faster depletion of oxygen. Practice in your performance clothes and shoes. This is especially important for a young woman who plans to wear heels or a dress with a tight waist. If the clothes and shoes interfere with the performance, wear something else.

The student should have at least four good concert-ready reeds, any of which you will feel comfortable performing upon. These reeds should be in place and feeling good seven to ten days before the concert. If at all possible, select these reeds by playing them in the hall where you will be performing. Reeds respond differently in a recital hall than they do in a practice room. A reed that may feel a little stiff in a practice room may not feel that way onstage.

Do not practice constantly on these reeds for the week prior to the concert, as you do not want to wear them out. But at the same time, you want to keep the feel for each reed in your embouchure, so do not simply let them sit for a week and not play on them at all. Take all these reeds on stage with you.

A successful performance depends not only on the preparation of the music, but also on the preparation of the mind. Confidence is your

---

TEACHING TIP

A teacher sitting in the audience can help a student pick a reed that sounds good to the audience. A reed may sound different to the audience than it does to the performer onstage, particularly if the student is not accustomed to playing in a large space. A reed that feels loud and coarse might actually be perfect.

PREPARING FOR A SOLO PERFORMANCE

secret weapon and is of the utmost importance. You must walk on stage as if you own the stage. You must be of the mind-set that you, as the performer, are in charge and that you will not make a mistake.

Before setting foot onstage, find a quiet spot to sit down. Begin with your feet and work your way up your body, feeling each part of your body releasing all tension. Try not to think of the performance, or anything, for that matter, as your body is relaxing. Focus on a black screen in your mind's eye. Do this for about five minutes, or longer if needed, until you are completely relaxed. Just before you walk out onstage, take a deep cleansing breath. Then take another breath that is not quite as deep. Then a final breath. With each of these three breaths feel yourself relaxing more and more.

With regard to music preparation, if possible research the composition or the composer. What was happening in the composer's life when he or she wrote the composition? Approach the music the same way as if you were preparing program notes. Record a rehearsal and study the recording with the score. Pay particular attention to ensemble precision, balance, and intonation.

Is the style correct for the time period of the piece in both the solo and the accompaniment? Can you hear the differences in legato, staccato, and normal tonguing? Can you identify the phrase endings and dynamics? Are ornamentations clean and consistent in both the solo and the accompaniment? Of course, all of this is in addition to having learned the piece properly and with the correct tempos.

If you are not sure of the style, tempos, or how to perform particular ornaments, find three recordings of the work by well-known clarinetists, not some student you find on YouTube. Compare the recordings. How do interpretations differ? Do you like one performance better than another?

If you are listening to a recording simply for interpretation, you may want to listen to the recording after you have put your own spin on the work, unless you do not know how to interpret the work. The idea of listening to recordings by famous clarinetists is not to copy what they are doing, but to get ideas on interpretation, style, etc., and incorporate those that you like from a number of different sources into your work.

When you walk onstage, you should take your position, smile, acknowledge your accompanist, and then bow. There is no hurry to begin playing; the audience will wait. Check to be sure your music stand is in the correct position and at the correct height and angle. Take a tuning pitch from the piano even if you tuned backstage. This gives you a moment to feel your tone in the space. Look at your music, make sure your pages are in order, and then make eye contact with the accompanist.

If you begin the piece on the downbeat, exhale, hear the opening in your mind at the correct tempo, inhale in tempo while giving the accompanist a good upbeat, and begin. If the accompanist begins and you enter a few measures later, you must nod to your accompanist to give the signal when you are ready to begin.

Do not forget at the end of your performance to bow. Bow at the waist and look at your shoes saying *one clarinet, two clarinet*, then stand up straight and look at the audience. Be sure not to bow and look at the audience while you are bowing; this looks like a marionette. Smile and acknowledge the accompanist.

When you walk offstage, keep an ear to the stage door. You may be called back for a second bow. If the applause is still going strong about five seconds after you leave the stage, go back out for a second bow, bringing your accompanist with you. Do not walk on for a second bow sheepishly, but do so proudly. After all, you have worked hard and deserve it.

ADVANCED

If playing in a jazz band where the audience may applaud after you have played an improvised solo, simply nod your head in appreciation to the audience as it would be inappropriate to take a full bow while the ensemble is still performing.

⑫

TEN STEPS TO
BETTER SIGHT-READING

Becoming a better sight reader involves actually reading new, never before seen literature. It may seem paradoxical to practice this skill. There are, however, some techniques the student can use to become a better sight reader. The following ten steps are referenced by corresponding numbers on the piece at the end of this chapter titled "Variations on Yankee Doodle." The piece is presented first without references in figure 12.1, and then with the following references, in figure 12.2.

1. *Title and Composer.* Make note of the title of the composition as it can give you an idea of the tempo or form of the composition. In this example, notice that the piece is going to have at least some thematic reference to the tune "Yankee Doodle." The tempo therefore will also probably be the tempo of that familiar tune. If, for example, the title has the word *jig* in it, then the tempo will be that of a lively dance. An *aria* or *largo* will be slow and lyrical; an *allegro* will be fast, a *march* highly rhythmic and accented, and so on.

    It is also important to look at the composer's name. If the composer is J. S. Bach or G. F. Handel, then the work is from the

Baroque period. This will give insight into the performance style of the piece, such as starting trills on the upper note of the trill. If the composer is Duke Ellington, then the piece will most likely be in jazz style and probably will use a swing eighth note. (Though not all jazz will always use a swing eighth note.)

2. *Key signature, time signature, and tempo.* The next item to scan for is the key signature, time signature, and any tempo markings. All too often a student will start sight-reading a piece only to think to himself/herself, *I really should have looked at the key signature, but now I don't dare take my eyes off the notes.* It has happened to all of us at some point. Take a moment to finger through the scale, particularly if it has three or more sharps or flats.

A tempo marking, particularly for a compound meter such as six-eight or nine-eight, is helpful in determining what type of note gets the pulse. If the tempo marking is allegro or moderato, then the dotted quarter note will generally get the pulse in a six-eight or nine-eight time. If the tempo marking is slow, such as largo or adagio, then the eighth note may well get the pulse.

3. *Rhythm.* When scanning the body of the work, look for any difficult or odd rhythms, or places where the music gets very black on the page. It is usually rhythmic difficulties that cause sight-reading to break down. Take a few seconds to think through the rhythms, fingering through them on your horn without playing, or tongue the rhythms silently with your tongue.

4. *Technical spots and accidentals.* Next scan the work for any technically challenging spots or any spots with accidentals. It may be necessary to slowly finger through any technical spots. This is where knowing major and minor scales and thirds comes in handy. Also, scan for any sudden leaps in register. If there are any high notes that may take you by surprise, make sure to count the leger lines and know what the pitch is and how to finger it.

5. *Articulations.* Articulations are often overlooked during sight-reading, although these are important musical features. In the course of scanning the composition, make note of any unusual slurs, accents, staccato, or legato markings.

6. *Dynamics.* A major musical element in any musical composition is the use of dynamics. Scan the work for the softest and the loudest spots. Do not forget about crescendos and diminuendos as these are very important and help shape the musical line.
7. *Symbols.* Try to notice any grace notes, turns, trills, DC and DS signs, repeats, codas, fermatas, and the like. If need be, grace notes, turns, and trills can be left off during sight-reading. Of course, it is best if you play these as they are as much a part of the music as everything else, but it is better to leave off a turn than to mess up a rhythm and get lost. If the band is sight-reading, be sure everyone knows if you are or are not going to take repeats and where the repeats go. It is best to take DCs, DSs, and codas, as these are important features of form.
8. *Tempo changes.* Watch for tempo changes such as *accelerandos*, *rallentandos*, *ritards*, etc. It is important to make a mental note of where these tempo changes occur so that you can look at the conductor and be prepared to change speed.
9. *Patterns.* Look for patterns before you begin playing. Baroque music, for example, is often full of sequential patterns. In the example at the end of this chapter, measures 14–17 show a three leg or three-part sequence. Patterns are not limited to pitches. In the example, the rhythm of eighth-two sixteenths and two sixteenths-eighth appears five times.
10. *Form.* A somewhat more advanced area of sight-reading is being able to recognize form. If the work is in ABA form (such as a minuet), then you can expect to be playing the same material with which you started. If the work is in rondo form (ABACA), then you can expect the A material to return.

Last, but not least, when sight-reading, you must listen. Listening to not only yourself, but to what is going on around you is probably the most important part of sight-reading. Even if you are sight-reading a piece by yourself, listen for familiar melodic material, patterns, dynamics, articulations, and of course the key in which you are playing. Be careful to listen to what you are actually playing, not what you think you are playing. This is a difficult skill for many students.

TEACHING TIP

If the band is sight-reading in a contest situation and there is time to talk through the piece, begin by conducting the piece. Have the students follow along in their parts without playing, as the director conducts. The director should hum the melody in rhythm interrupting himself/herself by calling out spots where cues to particular sections for entrances, melody changes, and so on, will take place. Point out any tricky rhythms. To ensure the students focus during this read-through, have them tap their own rhythm on their knees.

Figure 12.1. "Variations on Yankee Doodle," Arr. Brent Coppenbarger

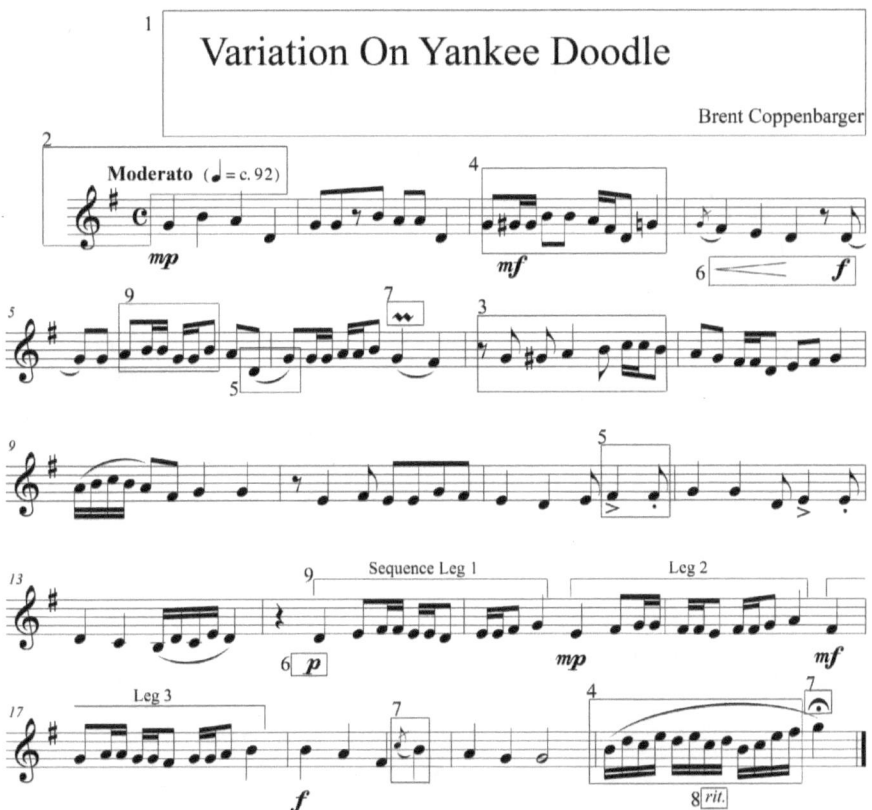

Figure 12.2. "Variations on Yankee Doodle" with References

CONCLUSION

It is important that students have fun playing their instruments. The better a student plays, the more fun he or she will have. A student who struggles with tone, intonation, embouchure issues, correct fingerings, etc. may soon lose interest in music. Music can be a lifelong endeavor if cultivated early, and it is the job of the band director to cultivate this talent. Some of the suggestions made throughout this handbook may be of use with other sections within the band.

The attempt has been made to reach as wide an audience as possible with this handbook, from the first-year teacher to the experienced teacher, to the student who wants to learn more about clarinet playing. Some information may be obvious to the experienced teacher, but perhaps not to the first-year teacher or the student. The concepts presented have been general in their scope. No attempt has been made to go into such detail as one would with, say, a college clarinet major. That was not the intent of this book.

There are many good books on the market for those clarinetists who want the specific details one will receive in a private clarinet lesson. Some of those books are listed in the appendix, along with suggestions of solos, études, and recordings for the more advanced clarinetist or for the teacher who may want to suggest material for his or her students. The intention with this handbook is simply to help improve the clarinet section and heighten interest in the clarinet through information that may make the clarinet more accessible to students.

APPENDIX

ADDITIONAL MATERIALS FOR CLARINETISTS

BOOKS

Blum, David. *Casals and the Art of Interpretation.* Berkeley and Los Angeles: University of California Press, 1977. This is a good book for those who would like some insights into thinking melodically about music.

Brymer, Jack. *Clarinet.* Kahn & Averill Publishers, 2001. This is a helpful reference book for advanced clarinetists.

Coppenbarger, Brent. *Music Theory Secrets: 94 Strategies for the Starting Musician.* Rowman & Littlefield, 2014. Designed for the student who has no music theory background, this book gives easy-to-understand explanations and memory tricks for a first-year music theory course. It can also be used by a music teacher as a guidebook for teaching music theory.

Gingras, Michèle. *Clarinet Secrets: 52 Performance Strategies for the Advanced Clarinetist.* Scarecrow Press, 2006. This is a great book for the serious student who wants some advanced technique strategies. Ms. Gingras is not only a master teacher, but a master performer as well. Look for her CDs.

Gingras, Michèle. *More Clarinet Secrets: 100 Quick Tips for the Advanced Clarinetists.* Scarecrow Press, 2011. Well worth reading.

Mazzeo, Rosario. *The Clarinet: Excellence and Artistry.* Dorn Publications, 1990. This book is based on the master class series Mazzeo wrote for the *Selmer Bandwagon* magazine. It is very detailed and a must-have for the serious clarinetist.

Pino, David. *The Clarinet and Clarinet Playing*. Dover Publications, 1998. In this book, Mr. Pino talks about equipment, the history of the clarinet, and how to teach clarinetists, among other subjects.

Stein, Keith. *The Art of Clarinet Playing*. Alfred Music, 1958. This is a good book for the intermediate clarinetist wishing to advance.

Thurston, Frederick. *Clarinet Technique*. Oxford University Press, 1985. This book covers many areas of concern to the clarinetist. It also has a good repertoire list in the back. This series also has a book on *Flute Technique* and *Oboe Technique*.

ETUDE BOOKS FOR THE ADVANCED CLARINETIST

Bona, Pasquale. *Complete Method for Rhythmical Articulation*. Kalmus. A good book, Bona makes one think about complicated rhythms.

Baermann, Karl. *Method for Clarinet, Third Division*, Carl Fischer Publishers. This is the standard scale method for the student studying privately.

Cavallini, Ernesto. *30 Caprices for Clarinet*. Various Publishers. This is college-level material for the advanced clarinetist.

Klose, Hyacinthe. *Daily Studies for the Clarinet*. Various Publishers. There are a number of studies by Klose. All are good finger and articulation studies that are fun to play.

Klose, Hyacinthe. *20 Studies for Clarinet*. Various Publishers.

Paisner, Ben. *19 Swing Etudes for Clarinet*. Sam Fox Publications. These are fun, intermediate etudes in swing style that can be used to introduce the student to this style.

Polatschek, Victor. *Advanced Studies for the Clarinet*. G. Schirmer. Some of these studies are difficult. What is unique about these studies is that Polatschek will write a study in the style of a particular composer or a composer's work. For example, Shostakovich, Symphony No. 1.

Rose, Cyrille. *32 Etudes for Clarinet*. Carl Fischer Publishers. This is the standard etude book for the student taking private lessons.

Rose, Cyrille. *40 Etudes for Clarinet*. Carl Fischer Publishers. Generally, the *40 Etudes*, available in two books, come after the *32 Etudes* with regard to a clarinetist's study.

Shaw, Artie. *Artie Shaw's Jazz Technique*. Warner Bros. Publications. The work is available in two books: Book one deals with scales, book two consists of fourteen etudes of medium difficulty that introduces the student to jazz style.

Uhl, Alfred. *48 Studies for Clarinet*. Schott Music. Book one is playable by a good high school clarinetist. Book two is difficult.

ADDITIONAL MATERIALS FOR CLARINETISTS

Voxman, Himie. *Classical Studies for Clarinet*. Rubank Publications. This book is playable by a good high school clarinetist. It uses works by Bach and Handel, thus it is Baroque literature, a style to which the clarinetist is not usually exposed.

Wine, Toby. *1001 Blues Licks*. Cherry Lane Music. Distributed by Hal Leonard Corp. This is a fun book consisting of many Blues styles in the twelve bar blues format. Each style has several pages of the first four bars, then several pages for the next four bars, then several pages of riffs for the last four bars. The student picks a lick from each set of pages, giving a vast number of available combinations. These are playable from about eighth grade on, with some licks more advanced than others. Be sure to get the treble clef book and not the bass clef.

MAGAZINES

The Clarinet. International Clarinet Association. This is a great magazine about what is happening in the clarinet world, available only to members of the International Clarinet Association, well worth joining (www.clarinet.org).

Instrumentalist Magazine. Instrumentalist Publishing. This magazine is a must for teachers in the music industry (www.instrumentalistmagazine.com).

RECORDINGS (LISTED BY PERFORMER)

Daniels, Eddie. *Memos from Paradise*. GRP Records, GRD-9561. Eddie Daniels is one of the great clarinetists of our time. His clean, crisp technique is a must to hear. He is primarily known as a jazz clarinetist, but has recorded standard *classical* literature as well. Any recording by Eddie Daniels is worth having in your library.

DeFranco, Buddy. *Born to Swing*. Hindsight Records, HCD701. This recording is a good introduction to jazz for the student clarinetist. Buddy DeFranco is one of the all-time great jazz clarinetists.

Fountain, Pete. *A Touch of Class*. Ranwood Records, MSD 35808. For examples of Dixieland style, any recording by Pete Fountain is a must have.

Gingras, Michèle. *Klassical Klezmer*. MSR Classics, 1240. This is a good introduction to the clarinetist who is interested in the Klezmer style. Ms. Gingras has a number of fine recordings available. Google her and check out her web site.

Leister, Karl. *Mozart Clarinet Concerto*. EMI Records, CDM 7 690142. This is Leister at his best playing with the Berlin Philharmonic with Herbert von Karajan conducting.

Marcellus, Robert. *Mozart Clarinet Concerto*. CBS Records, MYK 37810. This is considered *the* recording of the Mozart Clarinet Concerto. It should be in the library of every serious clarinetist.

Neidich, Charles. *Weber: Clarinet Concertos, Concertino*. Deustche Grammophon, 435 875-2. Charles Neidich has great technique and gives an inspiring performance on this CD. He has recorded a number of works, all worth having.

Stoltzman, Richard. *The Essential Clarinet*. RCA Victor, 09026-61360-2. This is a great recording of the Copland Concerto, the Corigliano Concerto, and the Bernstein Prelude, Fugue, and Riffs. Any recordings by Richard Stoltzman are well worth having.

SELECTED SOLOS FOR THE MORE ADVANCED CLARINETIST

A number of publishers are available in many cases.

Michael Bergson (1820–1898), *Scene and Air from Luisa de Montfort for Clarinet & Piano*. A fun piece and an audience favorite.

Luciano Berio (1925–2003), *Lied* for unaccompanied clarinet.

Leonard Bernstein (1918–1990), *Sonata for Clarinet & Piano*. Jazzy sounding and fun to play, it is one of my favorites.

Eugene Bozza (1905–1991), any of his many works for clarinet. His clarinet compositions tend to be on the difficult side.

Johannes Brahms (1833–1897), *Sonata No. 1 for Clarinet & Piano*, *Sonata No. 2 for Clarinet & Piano*. Standard repertoire for any serious clarinetist. These are great pieces requiring not only technical skill, but musical skill as well.

Aaron Copland (1900–1990), *Concerto for Clarinet*. Written for Benny Goodman. A great work that is somewhat difficult.

Bernhard H. Crusell (1775–1838). Any of his three clarinet concerti. My edition of his Concerto No. 1 is published by Musical Rara, now owned by Breitkopf and Härtal.

Claude Debussy (1862–1918), *Premiere Rhapsodie for Clarinet, Petite Piece for Clarinet & Piano.* The Premiere Rhapsodie is one of my favorite pieces. I have recorded it on my *Reeding Time* CD which is available on CDBaby.com.

Gerald Finzi (1901–1956), *Concerto for Clarinet, Five Bagatelles.*

Paul Hindemith (1895–1963), *Concerto for Clarinet, Sonata for Clarinet & Piano.* The sonata is the easier of the two works.

Witold Lutoslawski (1913–1994), *Dance Preludes for Clarinet & Piano.* A series of fun short pieces.

Felix Mendelssohn (1807–1847), *Sonata for Clarinet & Piano.* Not one of the stronger sonatas for clarinet and piano, but worth owning.

Wolfgang Amadeus Mozart (1756–1791), *Concerto for Clarinet, K. 622.* Composed in the last year of his life for his friend Anton Stadler, this is a standard work for all clarinetists and a must in the repertoire of any serious clarinetist.

Willson Osborne (1906–1979), *Rhapsody for Unaccompanied Clarinet.* Originally written for bassoon, this piece also works well for clarinet.

Gabriel Pierné (1863–1937), *Canzonetta for Clarinet & Piano, Op. 19.*

Francis Poulenc (1899–1964), *Sonata for Clarinet & Piano.* A very fine work and one of my favorites. Technically challenging.

Camille Saint-Saens (1835–1921), *Sonata for Clarinet & Piano, Op. 167.* Very French sounding, part of the standard repertoire.

Robert Schumann (1810–1856), *Fantasiestücke for Clarinet & Piano, Op. 73.* A good piece that clarinetists should know.

Ludwig Spohr (1784–1859), any of his four concerti for clarinet. The first concerto has the clarinet going up to high C; that is five leger lines plus a space.

Johann Stamitz (1717–1757), *Concerto in Bb.* Stamitz only wrote one clarinet concerto. He was the father of Karl Stamitz and a famous conductor of the Mannheim Orchestra.

Karl Stamitz (1746–1801), any of his eleven clarinet concerti.

Charles Stanford (1852–1924), *Sonata for Clarinet & Piano, Op. 129. Concerto for Clarinet, Op. 80.*

Antoni Szalowski (1907–1973), *Sonatina for Clarinet & Piano*. A fun piece to play and a good filler piece on a recital.

Carl Maria von Weber (1786–1826), *Concerto No. 1*, *Concerto No. 2*, *Concertino*, *Grand Duo Concertant Op. 48*. Standard repertoire for clarinetists. Fun pieces to play that are very impressive technically and musically.

Alec Wilder (1907–1980), *Sonata for Clarinet & Piano*.

I could go on and on listing more difficult works by Stravinsky, Martinu, Milhaud, Nielson, Tomasi, and others. It is like eating peanuts, you can't stop. But perhaps this list is at least a starting point to find literature for solo and ensemble, a solo with the band, recital repertoire, and other performances.

INDEX

Italicized page numbers indicate illustrations.

accent, 44, 49, 63–65, 70, 83
accidental, 94
accompaniment, 65, 91
advanced tips, 14, 20, 43, 50, 65, 83, 92
African blackwood, 19
air column, 11–12
air pressure, 7, 27, 35, 44–46, 49, 78
air pressure gauge, 35
air speed, 77
altissimo, 6, 15, 36, 41, 47, 80
angle, 6–8, 29, 53, 77, 92
articulation, 42–43, 45, 82–83, 85, 94; in exercises, 47, 57, 69

barrel, 24, 33–34, 36–38
bass clarinet, 78, 85
bassoon, 78–79, 83, 85
bassoonist, 2, 79
beginner tips, 6, 13, 20, 26, 34, 45, 54, 62, 76, 81–82, 86, 88

Bernoulli effect, 11
blues scale, 69, *70*
breath, 43, 82, 86, 90–91; mark, 87; pulse, 50–51; support, 35, 64, 76, 82
breathe, 68, 81, 86
Buffet, 19

cadence, 64, 86
case, 21, 27, 30–31
chalumeau register, 6, 16
chin, 4, 6–7, 79
chords, 68, *69*; seventh, 68; triad, 68
clarion register, 6
contact cement, 28–29
cork, 25, 27–29, 76, 84–85; bevel edge, 29
cork grease, 25
cork pads, 20
corners, 4, 6–8, 77

crescendo, 36, 49, 63–64, 95
crow: bassoon, 78; oboe, 77
cut, 12–13, 16

dampen, 3
density, 4–5, 12, 19
diminuendo, 36, 49, 63, 65, 95
disturbance time, 11
double lip. *See* embouchure
doubler, 2

einschnitt, 87
embouchure, 1–9, 23, 34–36, 38, 45, 50, 82, 84, 86; bassoon, 78; double lip, 1–2, 46; flute, 76–77; oboe, 77; saxophone, 79–80; single lip, 1–2

fingerings, 59–60
fingering technique, 56
flute: dynamics, 85; intonation, 76–77. *See also* embouchure
fulcrum, 2–4, 34

grace notes, 83
granadilla wood, 19

high notes, 15–16, 36, 41, 55, 77, 84, 94

instrument case. *See* case
instrument inspection check list, 30–31
intonation, 20, 24, 33–34, 37, 47, 55, 72, 75, 78; bassoon, 78; chart, 39; flute, 76–77; oboe, 77; saxophone, 79

jaw position, 8

key signature, 94
kinetic phrases, 63

lay, 2, 22
Leblanc, 19
lemon juice, 26
ligature, 14, 22–23
lower lip, 2–5, 7, 34; oboe, 77

melody, 62–63, 85, 96
meter, 70, 94
mouthpiece, 2–3, 7–8, 11, 13–16, 21–23, 26, 34, 36, 84, 88; jazz, 81; saxophone, 79, 81
Mpingo wood, 19
muscles, 5, 7–8; abdominal, 64

neck strap, 54, 84

oboe, 83, 85; intonation, 77
oil, 26, 85
oral cavity, 5, 42, 45
ornament, 63–64
ornamentation, 66
overbite, 78
overblow, 20

pad, 15, 20, 26–28, 84–85
Parafilm M, 7
Patricola, 19
patterns, 88, 95
performance, 89–92
phrase, 50, 56, 61, 63–65, 83, 86–87
pitch, 3, 6, 22, 34, 36, 42, 45, 76–77, 79–80, 86. *See also* intonation
placement: embouchure, 2, 3; teeth, 7; tongue, 5, 43. *See also* tongue position
plastic, 20–21, 30, 37
posture, 44, 75
practice, 5, 38, 44–46, 56–58, 89–90; record, 38; self-assessment, 39

INDEX

pressure, 3, 5, 7, 22, 34–35, 43, 45, 46, 78, 85

reed, 2–6, 11, 23, 26, 34, 36, 81, 90; articulation of, 43–36; bassoon, 78–79; break-in, 14–15; fuzzy tone, *16*; heart, 16; new, 13; oboe, 77; polishing, 14; rails, 12, 16; saxophone, 79–80, 84; sealing, 13; wavy, 16
replace torn tenon. *See* tenon
rest, 81, 87
rhythm, 50, 70, 81–82, 94–96; dotted, 70, 81–82; triplet figure, 70, 81–82
rosewood, 19
rubber band, 6–7, 27

saxophone, 80–85, 87; doubling, 78; intonation, 79; vibrato, 80
Selmer, 19, 101
sight-reading, 94–96
single lip. *See* embouchure
skin pad, 20. *See also* pad
solo, 64–65, 89
soloist, 65
staccato, 43–44, 56, 83
standing, 44, 54, 84, 90
swab, 25–26
symbols. *See* ornamentation

syncopation, 70, 83
synthetic, 24, 33

teaching tips, 7, 15, 22–23, 27, 30, 35, 44, 55, 58, 72, 76–77, 79, 82, 85, 90, 96
tempo, 47, 53, 62, 93–95
tenon, 27, 37; replace, 28–29
throat tone, 20, 36, 85
tone, 1, 3, 11, 19, 21, 33–35, 80–81; drone, 73; hole, 52–53; voicing of, 36; while tonguing, 45–46
tongue position, *48*
toothpick, 27
trill, 54–55, 94
twelve-bar blues, 69

upper lip, 2, 5, 7, 78

vamp, 13
"Variations on Yankee Doodle," *96–97*
vascular bundles, 12, 14, 16
vibrational speed, 3, 11
vibrato, 63, 80

warble, 27
warm up, 34; chorale, 72
weather, 75
woodwinds, 75

Yost excerpt, *51*

ABOUT THE AUTHOR

Brent Coppenbarger is professor of music at the Cline School of Music at North Greenville University, where he has taught single reeds, music theory, and various other music classes since 1995. He has been a freelance musician in Wisconsin, Virginia, and South Carolina, having played bass clarinet in the Carolina Pops Orchestra, principal clarinet in the Greenville Opera Company, and principal clarinet in the Beloit-Janesville Symphony Orchestra, and has subbed as clarinetist in the Greenville Symphony Orchestra.

Dr. Coppenbarger received his doctor of musical arts degree in clarinet performance from the University of Wisconsin–Madison School of Music. He has a master of music degree in performance from the Chicago Music College of Roosevelt University and a bachelor of music degree in performance from the University of Wisconsin–Whitewater. His articles have appeared in the *Instrumentalist Magazine*, *The Clarinet* (Journal of the International Clarinet Association), and *NACWPI Journal* (National Association of College Wind & Percussion Instructors).

Dr. Coppenbarger has had a number of original compositions and arrangements published by Dorn Publications, and his edition of the *Bernhard Crusell Concerto in E-flat, Op. 1, No. 1* for clarinet and piano is published by Musica Rara, now owned by Breitkopf and Härtal. His

CD, *Reeding Time*, with his wife, Sonja, playing bassoon, can be found on CDBaby.com. It features children's stories rewritten by Ms. Coppenbarger with musical accompaniment composed by Dr. Coppenbarger. Dr. Coppenbarger is also author of *Music Theory Secrets: 94 Strategies for the Starting Musician* (Rowman & Littlefield, 2014).

www.ingramcontent.com/pod-product-compliance
Lightning Source LLC
Chambersburg PA
CBHW030145240426
43672CB00005B/279